NADIA

a case of extraordinary
drawing ability
in an autistic child

NADIA

*a case of
extraordinary
drawing ability
in an autistic
child*

Lorna Selfe

ACADEMIC PRESS

London · New York · San Francisco

1977   A Subsidiary of Harcourt Brace Jovanovich, Publishers

ACADEMIC PRESS INC. (LONDON) LTD
24–28 Oval Road
London NW1

U.S. Edition published by
ACADEMIC PRESS INC
111 Fifth Avenue
New York, New York 10003

LCCCN 76–22839
ISBN 0–12–635750–1

PRINTED IN GREAT BRITAIN BY
WILLIAM CLOWES AND SONS LTD
LONDON, BECCLES AND COLCHESTER

Preface

This book is the result of a practical case study undertaken at the Child Development Research Unit, University of Nottingham, and completed in September 1974. Nadia was far too interesting and remarkable a child to go unnoticed or unrecorded. John and Elizabeth Newson were of the same opinion and Anthony Watkinson of Academic Press also recognized that we had discovered a rare, if not unique, case.

Nadia aged 6½ years

I hope that this book will be of interest to psychologists, art teachers and artists, to teachers generally, to those working in the field of mental handicap and to all those who like to be astonished! As a practising educational psychologist I have only a lay knowledge of art and aesthetics and I hope that artists and art teachers will be tolerant of any naivety that I show of their field.

The case study is written in two distinct sections. The first half is a description of Nadia, her history and her drawing habits. These chapters will be of general interest. In the chapters following the drawings I have considered her ability from the standpoint of established psychological studies. A physiological explanation for Nadia's phenomenal drawing ability is considered and I have included all the psychological test results which I was able to obtain. These chapters will probably be of greater interest to psychologists, but I hope that other readers will not be deterred.

v

In the course of my studies I have benefited from the work of three writers in particular. Helga Eng's study of her niece, Margaret, illustrated for me clarity of format and exposition. Dale Harris' work on children's drawing ability as measures of intellectual maturity was used to gain comparisons of Nadia's ability with normal development. I found myself much in sympathy with Harris and Eng's emphasis on the role of conceptual and cognitive development in children's drawings. Susanne Langer's philosophical work on symbolic logic provided me with a theoretical framework and insights into the conceptual processes taken for granted by Eng and Harris. Langer emphasizes the role of conceptualization or "symbolization" in human thought and differentiates between discursive (linguistic) and presentational (mental imagery) forms. Her work has illuminated my understanding of the whole area and as a result I am engaged in a further analysis of her theories.

I have been particularly lucky to have had the wise and humane guidance of John and Elizabeth Newson. I am also deeply indebted to Nicholas Parsons and Antonia Cowan whose helpful criticism and advice has been invaluable. Their intellectual tenacity, tempered with humour, have done much to sharpen my own awareness.

I would like to acknowledge my debt to Nadia's family, for their hospitality and helpfulness whilst I was studying Nadia, and for their permission for this publication. I am also grateful to several colleagues with whom I discussed aspects of the text; especially Dr A Buffery, Dr G Dutton, Mr R Moseley and Dr G Simon. Finally, I am especially indebted to Ms Jane Duncan of Academic Press who has given me invaluable assistance in turning my original study into this book.

This book is dedicated to Nadia who has taught me so much. I should like to feel that my study goes some way to establish Nadia's extraordinary ability; although the drawings have their own eloquence, mocking ordinary descriptions. Since the study was completed, I have had many discussions with experts in the field and my belief in the extraordinary nature of the case has only been strengthened.

Recently, I have been pleased to notice a growing interest in single case studies. I hope that this study may be in the vanguard. I should like to begin my book with Luria's words at the end of his study of "S" (the case of a mnemonist):

Psychology has yet to become a science that is capable of dealing with the really vital aspects of human personality . . . The development of such a psychology is a job for the future, and at present it is difficult to say how many decades it will be before we achieve it . . . But there is no doubt that research into the way an imbalance of individual aspects of development affects the formation of personality structure . . . will constitute one important method of the approaches used.

Lorna Selfe   *August 1977*

Contents

Preface   v

Introduction by Elizabeth Newson   1

1. Nadia: Her Family and Background   3
    Nadia   3
    Family background   3
    History from birth until 1974   4
    Reports of Nadia's development   5

2. Nadia's Drawing Ability   8
    Drawing behaviour   8
    Line   8
    Timing   8
    Time spent in drawing   9
    Space   9
    Colour   9
    Subject matter   9

3. The Drawings   11
    Further experimental investigation of Nadia's ability   13
    Analysis of drawing by use of Video-film   13

Drawings 1–106   16–95

4. Comparisons   98
    A comparison of Nadia's ability with established empirical findings   98
    Comparison with the drawing ability of normal children   99
    Comparison with the drawing ability of deaf children   106
    Comparison with the drawing ability of mentally retarded children   106
    Comparison with the drawing ability of autistic children   107
    Comparison with normal children of exceptional ability   107
    Comparison with mentally retarded children with special talents   107
    Theories of the "idiot savant"   109

5. A Consideration of Wider Theoretical Issues   110
    Wider issues   110
    Eidetic imagery and drawing ability   112

6. Physiological Considerations   114
    What are the facts relevant to a physiological explanation?   114

7. Cognitive Examination of Nadia   119
    Reynell Developmental Language Scale   119
    Pre-requisites of language development   120
    Special language impairment   122
    The Columbia Mental Maturity Scale   122
    Merrill–Palmer Mental Measurement of preschool children   .   .   .   122
    Other tests of mental maturity   123
    Frostig Developmental Test of visual perception   123
    General tests   123

8. Conclusions   125

Postscript by Elizabeth Newson   129

Drawings 107–109   131–133

References   135

Introduction by Elizabeth Newson

To marvel is the beginning of knowledge
and where we cease to marvel we may be in danger
of ceasing to know
             Gombrich

Gombrich's words are exquisitely pertinent to introduce Nadia, a child who turns upside down all our notions of graphic representation. How incredible we found her, when we first saw her at the Child Development Research Unit at the University of Nottingham, may perhaps be understood when I explain that, some years earlier, we had been the fortunate inheritors of 24,000 "pictures of mummy", the results of a children's competition in the *Observer*. We had spent some time analysing these drawings and paintings in terms of the stages of development which characterize children's ability to depict the human form; we had, indeed, mounted an exhibition on the subject for the British Association for the Advancement of Science.* We thought we *knew* what was possible for a 6-year-old, and what was not.

Nadia came into our lives without any warning of how she was to shatter our beliefs. Her mother had telephoned me one January afternoon: a mild, slightly apologetic voice with a strong Ukrainian accent. She was worried about her 6-year-old daughter; the child had almost no speech, and was attending a local special school for severely subnormal children, where she seemed to be making no progress. A neighbour had suggested she should approach Sutherland House, the Nottingham school for autistic children, and the head teacher there had advised her to contact me. Could I help?

I offered to see Nadia in my weekly clinic, and there she arrived three weeks later with her mother and little sister: a slow-moving, solidly built little girl with a distant smile, who appeared to accept the novel experience of our playroom with passivity rather than interest. In this clinic we use an integrated team approach: one person, working with the child in the playroom, attempts to "discover" the child to the rest of the team, consisting of several observers, the parents, and myself as co-ordinator, who sit together in the twilight of the observation room, separated from the playroom by the one-way screen which takes up the whole wall. In this way we learn about the child from two sources at once: both from what we see through the screen, and from the parent's account of the child's past and present history, elicited by detailed questioning and stimulated by the visual aid that the child provides.†

Lorna Selfe happened to be the psychologist working in the playroom on this occasion; Nadia's mother talked to me about the child. Early on in the conversation, she said that she had brought along a few drawings that Nadia had done: maybe I would be interested? I said I should love to see them presently, and we continued to talk about Nadia's babyhood. Meanwhile Nadia, on the other side of the screen, had been presented with the fat wax crayons which seemed to be suitable to the general level of play and manipulative competence that she had shown so far, and was scrubbing away at the paper to produce a formless yellow

* Exhibition entitled "The Innocent Eye", now available as an illustrated audiotape from the Medical Recording Service Foundation, Kitts Croft, Writtle, Chelmsford, Essex.
† Newson, Elizabeth, "Parents as a resource in diagnosis and assessment", in Oppé, T., and Woodford, P. (ed.) (1976). "Early Management of Handicapping Disorders", Elsevier, Excerpta Medica, Amsterdam.

scribble. How were we to know that her chosen medium was ballpoint, and that her performance was obsessionally dependent upon the right materials being offered her?

We started to talk about the things Nadia liked doing at home, and her mother rummaged in her bag and produced a small bundle of half-a-dozen drawings. I looked at them in the half-light: rather faint blue lines on poor-quality paper. I went through the little pile again. When I did speak, I was aware of the banality of the remark in comparison to my confused thoughts: "These are really very good", I think it was. But Nadia's mother knew she had made her point; by the time they went home, we had photocopied every one in triplicate.

My first reaction to the drawings was to marvel; my second, I am ashamed to say, to doubt. In the conference that followed the clinic, there was general agreement among the observers (none of whom had seen the drawings) that Nadia's level of ability as evidenced by what we had seen in the playroom was very low. At this point the photocopies were handed round, and were examined minutely, at first in stunned silence, then in a hubbub. The consensus hardened: "She's having you on, Elizabeth, it's *not possible* for any 6-year-old to draw like that". Reluctantly, I began to agree; it was even more traumatic for me to think that in my carefully planned clinic setting a parent might have lied to me in cold blood, than to have my "understanding" of children's drawing upset—yet clearly the drawings were *not possible*. Lorna finally said, without much hope, that if they did turn out to be authentic she would make a protracted study of this child. A few days later, Nadia showed her . . .

1

Nadia: Her Family and Background

Nadia

Nadia was born in Nottingham to Ukrainian emigré parents on 24 October 1967. She was the second-born child in a family of three children. Although the development of the other two children was normal—and they were bilingual—Nadia failed to develop language properly and the few words she had at nine months disappeared. Both her expressive language and comprehension of language were extremely poor and she was virtually mute. When Nadia's language failed to develop, the family adopted the policy of speaking to her in English—on the assumption that if she could only master one language it should be English.

I worked with Nadia from March to September, 1974 when she was $6\frac{1}{2}$ years of age, and was attending a local school for severely subnormal children. I observed her in regular two-hour sessions twice a week at school or in her home.

The over-riding impression of Nadia was of lethargy and impassivity. Physically, she was very large for her age and was clumsy, poorly co-ordinated and excessively slow in her movements. She was largely impassive to social approaches. Her vocabulary was limited to some ten single-word utterances heard over this five-month period. She did not respond to command or instruction and it was extremely difficult to know whether she merely did not comprehend or whether she was refusing to co-operate.

At $3\frac{1}{2}$ years of age, Nadia had suddenly displayed an extraordinary drawing ability. This was marked from the outset by a high level of skill, manual dexterity and quality so sadly absent in all other areas of her functioning. This ability (extremely rare in a child of this age, let alone for a child who had no language or was otherwise apparently functioning at a severely subnormal level) continued to develop over the next three years. I was fortunate to work with her during a very productive period.

Family Background

Nadia's father came to Britain from the Ukraine in 1947, with his mother—who always lived with the family. He is an electrical engineer and speaks English fluently.

Nadia's mother, who sadly died in 1975, came to Britain in 1964 from Poland to be re-united with close members of her family. She married shortly afterwards. She had obtained a Master's Degree in Chemistry in Poland and had been a teacher in her own country, before she emigrated, in her late thirties.

For five years before she died she worked full time as a laboratory technician at a local technical college. For the first four years of her marriage, when she did not work, she had little need to speak English—and indeed, later, her work situation did not encourage an extensive use of English. She attended evening classes twice a week to rectify this, but her command of the language remained poor.

Nadia's grandmother spoke no English, did not assimilate basic English habits and was much absorbed in her traditional culture. Since the death of Nadia's mother, she has assumed the role of housekeeper.

The family spoke Ukranian in the home and since the two other children (one older than Nadia, one younger) were bilingual, Nadia was effectively excluded from family conversations—although they did speak English to her.

There was no evidence of outstanding artistic ability in other members of the family.

History from Birth Until 1974

Nadia was born at home after a normal birth and uneventful pregnancy. She was of normal birthweight and there were no special features of immediate pre- and post-natal periods. However, development was slow. Her mother reported that she was "unlike other babies". She was unresponsive and would not turn at her mother's approach. When placed on her mother's lap she seemed to have poor muscle tone and leaned against her mother, not for comfort, but as if she could not sit up, and would droop her head and shoulders. There was no trouble with breast or bottle feeding and she was weaned at six months without any problems.

Nadia's first words appeared at nine months. She rapidly acquired about ten words in Ukrainian: Mama, Dada, Grandma, Goodnight, etc. When she was one year old her mother started her full time job. Nadia was cared for by her grandmother—a particularly quiet person, and Nadia's mother expressed regret that from this time the child did not have much language stimulation.

She stood with support at one year but did not walk alone until she was 2 years old. Holophrases and then two-word utterances, which normally appear at 18 months, did not develop and the single-word utterances she had acquired appeared less and less frequently. Her younger sister was born when Nadia was 20 months old. Nadia had a particularly bad attack of measles at the age of 2 years and had to remain in bed for a month. During this time she became increasingly emotionally isolated and her family first began to worry that her development was not proceeding normally. At $2\frac{1}{2}$ years she would run away to the park and seemed especially heedless of danger; she was inattentive and increasingly difficult to control. When Nadia was 3 years old, her mother entered hospital with breast cancer. In the months before hospitalization Nadia's mother was deeply despairing and later believed that she had neglected the child at that time.

The grandmother cared for the children throughout this harrowing period. Nadia was confined to her bedroom for long periods as the grandmother found it difficult to cope with her—and she did not visit her mother in hospital. On her mother's return, after three months, Nadia was overjoyed to see her. During her recuperation Nadia's mother had time to play with the child and it was at this time that Nadia began her drawings. From the start her mother was impressed by her dexterity and extraordinary ability.

When Nadia was $4\frac{1}{2}$ the local General Practitioner advised special education for her, to begin as soon as possible in the interest of remediation. She entered a Day Special School (Severely Sub Normal/SSN) in 1972.

The headmistress recalls that Nadia was toilet trained but could only eat with a spoon when she first started school. She was sometimes destructive and frequently had uncontrollable attacks of screaming. She was physically large for her age, but slow and lethargic in her movements. She was able to enter a normal class in the school and did not need special care or training. Her typical behaviour was of passivity and excessive slowness and as she was mute and inactive she was not a behaviour problem. Her teachers and headmistress soon discovered her drawing ability and gave her opportunities for drawing. Her talent was occasionally demonstrated to visitors.

Whilst Nadia was in her special school she made very little progress in language development and her effective vocabulary was less than ten words. She showed persistence with a wide range of perceptual motor toys and mastered many, such as shoe-lace threading toys, form boards, jig saws and the use of small apparatus in the gymnasium. She appeared to be content and generally integrated in the school although she had regular temper tantrums when she would scream and shout uncontrollably for two or three hours at a time.

Her typical behaviour in the classroom was one of withdrawal into her own private world with passive co-operation towards her teacher. She would sit for half an hour staring into space or wander slowly and aimlessly about the room. As she was excessively slow she rarely finished her school dinner. She obeyed in a passive manner and regularly had to be helped to put on her shoes or to open a door—although she had made a move in the right direction so showing that she had understood the command. She rarely initiated a social contact with another person other than those simple ones which would satisfy a basic need such as to indicate that she wished to go to the toilet. However, she developed a liking for another girl in her class whom she followed about and was often upset when the girl was out of the room.

At home Nadia's behaviour was very similar. She was generally co-operative and managed to indicate her needs by gesture and by leading by the hand. She had moods and bad temper tantrums when she was destructive and she occasionally smashed milk bottles and broke the fretwork on the piano. She displayed some jealousy of her younger sister. Nadia was very dependent on her mother and followed her about the house.

If the family went out for the day Nadia loved such visits and showed her pleasure by an increased generalized excitement. However, she was very slow and almost unsure on her feet, lagging behind the rest of the family who would have to stop frequently to allow her to catch them up. She ate well at home where she had plenty of time to finish her meals and she slept well, going to bed at 9.00 p.m.

Reports of Nadia's Development

At the age of 5 years 3 months Nadia was seen by a Senior Clinical Psychologist and the following extracts of his report are interesting.

> *Behaviour :* Nadia was seen at the end of a tiring day of Out-Patient appointments and was clearly anxious. Her mother was present during the interview. It was clear immediately that Nadia is a very disturbed girl who seemed big for her age and who showed a good deal of gaze-avoidance and some mannerisms. She engaged briefly in some symbolic play with a doll but ignored much of what was asked of her. Her mother told me that she is attending a special school in Nottingham but she wishes to have a further opinion and to be able to make educational plans. The picture is complicated by the fact that the family speak Ukrainian at home but Nadia was almost completely unresponsive when her mother spoke to her in Ukrainian. It seemed, in part, that some negativism accounted for this.
>
> *Testing :* Because Nadia was tired and anxious, formal assessment was not possible. She was, however, manifestly interested in a number of non-verbal tasks, especially form boards and simple puzzles. She showed a good capacity for shape recognition and made no errors on such tasks. This is consistent with skills at least for a four-year level. She also is able to produce exceptionally skilful drawings, particularly of horses, though these may not be creative as much as memories of pictures she has seen.
>
> In contrast, Nadia has very limited verbal skills that are probably not attributable to her family background. She showed some echolalia and produced one or two short phrases. Her understanding of speech is severely limited, though she has some.
>
> *Discussion :* Her language skills are severely retarded and in addition she shows a number of unusual features that indicate full psychiatric assessment.

One month later, a thorough psychological and medical examination was conducted at the Hospital for Sick Children, Great Ormond Street, London and extracts from this report are as follows.

> The results of the investigations on Nadia are now to hand. She is obviously an extremely interesting child. She is above the 97th percentile for height and weight and her bone age suggests that she is older than her years. We have not been able to put a specific diagnosis to her although her features suggest some autistic behaviour and possible considerable psychiatric disturbance.
>
> The results of her tests are as follows: full blood count within normal limits; E.S.R. 10; X-ray report of the skull, the vault is brachycephalic. The sella is somewhat small with a thick dorsum sellae. There is no intracranial calcification. Bone age is seven to eight years. Amino

acid and sugar chromatography; there is evidence of reducing substances in the urine and mild generalised amino acid urea. Urinary sugars; glucose 5 mg/100 ml, sucrose 60 mg/100 ml, fructose 20 mg/100 ml. The significance of these is uncertain and we shall be repeating the tests. The EEG report reads: This record shows only a slight excess of irregular intermediate slow activity and a few sharp elements in the resting record. However there is an abnormal response to photic stimulation at fast to flash rates. No obvious clinical changes were associated with this. The audiologist felt that her hearing was probably normal for routine speech. Our speech therapist thought that her features were somewhat autistic and although she could not put any specific label to Nadia's behaviour she was impressed by her exceptional drawing skills and felt that she required extensive language stimulation.

A number of interesting physiological factors are revealed by this report, together with the suggestion of autism, which are discussed later.

When Nadia was 6½ years of age she was taken to the Child Development Research Unit, Nottingham University, where she was seen by Dr Elizabeth Newson and two trainees. The following are relevant extracts from the report.

Present condition

Special senses

Visual : Nadia appears to have no difficulty in recognizing her parents or her own house. She often looks out of the corners of her eyes at things or people. She may move an object in front of her eyes in order to study it, but does not move her own head when fixating. Visual avoidance is only shown in response to a bright light—this she dislikes, and covers her eyes with her hands.

She seems very short-sighted, and her mother believes her to be so. She brings objects close to her eyes, and bends close over the paper when drawing. However, when looking at a book she holds it at a normal distance. She used often to fall over things or walk into things, and sometimes nearly does so now, but just misses them.

Auditory : She has been thought deaf because she is inattentive and non-responsive. She is now more responsive than in the past, i.e. intermittently so. She especially enjoys music, particularly piano music.

Other senses : No obvious anomalies shown.

Speech

Although her first words (in Ukrainian) appeared at nine months, no development of expressive language has taken place. Her experience up to age 2 was totally Ukrainian, it is believed, i.e. this was effectively a one-language home until some time after Nadia's speech was giving cause for concern. Her mother now uses Ukrainian for everyday conversation or instructions to her, i.e. going through books and naming objects in pictures. Nadia will not listen to stories.

Nadia can name objects in pictures, sometimes spontaneously, sometimes when prompted. She can use common two-word phrases she has heard, like "naughty boy", "take down", "come on", "go outside", "good girl", but cannot herself combine two words. There is some delayed echolalia used inappropriately. She can understand simple instructions like "get the biscuit off the table", but if the request is unusual like "put the brush on the window-sill", she becomes confused. She seems pleased when she understands, but shows no distress when she does not. Her mother thinks she is jealous of Tania's understanding. Nadia will normally lead an adult by the hand to get what she wants. Sometimes she manages on her own, i.e. when there wasn't enough milk on the table, she went to get some more.

When disturbed or confused she will suddenly talk jargon to herself—no one can understand what she says. She can sing a recognizable melody including a few words.

Dexterity

Nadia can dress herself but does not usually as she is very slow. She is liable to put her clothes on the wrong way round. She cannot manage buttons but can do up large press-studs. She can use a spoon or fork separately but not together, and cannot use a knife. She can unwrap a chocolate bar without dropping the chocolate.

The feature which overshadows every other characteristic is Nadia's drawing. She started drawing at 3 and seemed to her mother unusually skilled then; for a time she scribbled on walls but once she had plenty of paper she drew representationally.

Her drawing is inspired by pictures, and apparently sometimes solid objects which she has seen, but she does not have the model in front of her while drawing nor does she have to have seen it recently. Different versions of the same model seem very similar in detail, but it may be that she changes orientation and some of the details. She sometimes scribbles finely on parts of the model. Even if one posits the tracing of an eidetic image (which presents theoretical difficulties of time-span and image dimension), her motor co-ordination is quite incredibly fine for a *normal* child of this age. She draws very fast, can return to the exact point necessary on an interrupted line, may "finish" a picture and then return and add detail or decoration. Her drawing of, for example an eye, is exceptionally precise.

Gross motor behaviour

Other than in drawing, Nadia gives an impression of slowness, clumsiness and heaviness. She is a large, rather lethargic child. She will sit on a wheeled toy or rocking horse and enjoy this, but not actually set it in motion. When angry or frustrated, she will "stutter" with her feet, clench her teeth and hit out at a person or the piano, kick the door, shout—this happens most days but she returns to placidity. She has always been rather inactive.

Activities and play

Nadia's mother says she is seldom quite unoccupied. She draws at home, but not every day; likes to "play" the piano. She likes to play with water for the trickle of it on her fingers, but not constructively. She will look at a book with attention. She likes to sit on her mother's knee.

One slightly obsessive activity is to tear paper carefully into strips—this she does with any paper *except her drawings*. She throws the strips away.

Idiosyncratic

Mannerisms appear almost nil, other than the facial avoidance while fixating which results in her looking out of the corners of her eyes. She occasionally laughs to herself.

Resistance to change is shown in several ways. She dislikes there to be a change of expected events or of usual route. She is upset when she doesn't go to school. She is very pleased to have new clothes, but is distressed by the "wrong" combinations of clothes or if her shoes are left undone etc.—clothes have to be arranged just so. Her teddy bear and dolls are arranged in bed in special places, and she will replace them insistently if they are disarranged.

Nadia has no fear of ordinary dangers, and could not be trusted not to run into traffic or into a moving swing.

Comments

This extremely unusual child needs much more investigation. Her autistic features as they stand would probably not be sufficient to warrant a definite diagnosis of autism*; yet her quite extraordinary drawing ability, however it is eventually explained, shows the label of non-specific severe subnormality to be totally inadequate. It is hoped that intensive investigation of her one remarkable talent will begin to identify ways in which her potentialities in other directions can be maximized.

---

* The diagnosis of autism has in fact been substantiated over time. Nadia satisfies the criteria in terms of:

Impairment of social relationships : Unresponsive to her mother's approach as a baby, she has continued to seem detached socially, and to show that lack of social empathy which is particularly characteristic of autism. Relationships with other children now focus on an obsessional concern for their presence rather than on actual interaction with them.

Impairment of language : Language development proceeded very slowly indeed, and continued to show echolalia and ritualistic speech patterns.

Evidence of rigidity and inflexibility of thought processes, in particular shown by ritualistic behaviour. In addition to the ritualistic nature of Nadia's speech and her social behaviour, a compulsive feature that we did not appreciate when the report was written was the restriction of her drawing to one medium, i.e. ballpoint pen. This is the significance of her very poor performance under clinic conditions when given a wax crayon: although she used it on paper, she made no attempt to draw with it. Ballpoint remained her medium, although she was eventually persuaded (for filming purposes) to use a fibre pen occasionally. Resistance to change was noted at age 6, and Nadia remains distressed by changes in familiar school routine.

Early onset : The report shows onset of Nadia's condition well before the age of 30 months normally taken as the criterion: in particular her lack of social response in babyhood, failure to develop two-word utterances during the second and third years, and unusual heedlessness of danger at age 2 years.

Elizabeth Newson

2

Nadia's Drawing Ability

I witnessed Nadia drawing on many occasions during my work with her, and I was able to make a video tape of her drawing (see Fig. 1, pp. 30–31). Although, because communication was extremely difficult, she would seldom draw to order. She would not draw for social reward but very much according to her own intrinsic motivation. I was unable to discover the critical variables which would make her want to draw—although some factors were always present. She had to be in a happy and contented mood and usually in familiar surroundings. Food rewards usually upset the drawing performance.

From a layman's experience of children's and adult's drawings it was evident that Nadia had an exceptional ability. This ability can be carefully compared and contrasted with drawing ability of normal children of matched age (see Chapter 4, pp. 85, 96, 97). Nadia's drawings are qualitatively different from those of children of normal intelligence of her age in many respects, including proportion, perspective, manual dexterity, the iilusion of movement and foreshortening. This will be discussed in detail (p. 98) after the following description of the drawings and Nadia's method of executing them.

Drawing Behaviour

Nadia was lefthanded and held the biro between thumb and index finger, using her second finger for support in a competent and practised manner unlike the clumsy attitude of young children. She placed her face very close to the paper when she drew which suggested she might be myopic. (An appointment with an eye specialist however, confirmed that she did not need spectacles.) She generally drew swiftly and deftly, becoming animated—in marked contrast to her normal lethargic behaviour.

Line

Nadia used fine, quickly executed lines. Her motor control was highly developed, judged by her speed and the accuracy of execution together with a general deftness. She did not need to look at the line she had just drawn while surveying the movement of her hand at the same time—as is the case with many infants. Her lines were firm and executed without unintentional wavering. She could stop a line exactly where it met another despite the speed with which the line was drawn. She could change the direction of a line and draw lines at any angle towards and away from the body. She could draw a small but perfect circle in one movement and place a small dot in the centre.

Timing

She drew intensively for varying intervals of time but for not more than one minute. She usually sat back to survey the effect, moving her head perhaps, to vary the viewing angle.

This usually gave her great pleasure and after surveying intently what she had drawn she often smiled, babbled and shook her hands and knees in glee. However, it was at this point that she was most distractible and she could fall into a staring reverie perhaps lasting for several minutes before she continued drawing.

Time Spent in Drawing

Nadia enjoyed drawing and this was when she was most animated and lively. She drew for four or five sessions during the week. She could use up a large quantity of paper and the opportunity for drawing was sometimes restricted by lack of materials so it was difficult to ascertain how much she would draw if she had been presented continually with the opportunity to do so. She drew less frequently at school than at home.

Her motivation varied and in some sessions her drawings were quickly and sketchily executed and she would use up several sheets of paper in the course of a few minutes. On other days she would persist at one drawing for up to an hour. Her mother often gave her one sheet of paper at a time to encourage this persistence. Nadia occasionally returned to drawings done two or three days earlier to add lines—and she could spoil a drawing by repeated additions.

She would stop drawing abruptly, pushing the paper away even though the image might have been half completed, or often she lost interest because the continuation of the image she was drawing lay off the edge of the paper.

Space

Nadia would begin drawing at any point on the paper although usually at the middle to bottom. She never attempted to "squeeze" the shape or object on to the edge of the paper but would draw lines straight off the edge, sometimes dissecting and terminating the image at a vital spot—half a head—for instance. She evidently repressed or received no emotional satisfaction from completeness* but was dominated by the shape and appearance of the form.

Colour

She showed no interest in colour and did not attempt to colour any of her pictures although the drawings which inspired her were often highly coloured.

Subject Matter

It is important to emphasize that Nadia did not copy her drawings from pictures—although most of her drawings had originals. These were frequently taken from "Ladybird" children's books, newspapers, or wall prints (see Figs 2, 3, 4, 5 pp. 42, 43, 52), where the quality of the original was often crude or highly stylized.

When she first saw the originals, Nadia did not copy them, but studied them attentively and occasionally scribbled back and forth on their outlines. Her reproductions, which might appear a day or so later, were usually recognizable as versions of the original—but her image, although beautifully proportioned, could be a different size and occasionally completely reversed.

With practice and experimentation the image often changed. Her pictures of horses, for example, may have been a composite of the many horses she had observed and it was difficult

* See pp. 101–102.

to find originals since there were so many possibilities. In cases where the original has been found and where other sources can be safely ruled out we can see that she frequently distorted and transformed the original but often to render her drawing more interesting. The essential features and basic shape, however, were rarely destroyed, or so distorted as to leave the reproduction unrecognizable. A fascinating feature of her ability was that she paid attention to those features which normally receive most attention in the drawings of intelligent children—or in visual scanning, such as the face of the animal. The more complex details in terms of density of lines, such as hair or tail feathers were often given cursory treatment. From her limited cognitive understanding she somehow discerned those areas which required concentration and detailed study.

Nadia's mother stated on several occasions that she believed Nadia drew from life. I presented Nadia with many opportunities to do this using toys and live objects (including a visit to a zoo). However, there was only one occasion when I observed Nadia draw from life and this was a study of myself (see Drawing 89, p. 87), though I believe that the studies of shoes and legs were also inspired by observations from life as this is the only explanation for their range and variety (p. 88). Finally, it is important to reiterate that Nadia was never observed to refer to the original (either picture or life) once she began to draw.

3

The Drawings

It has been convenient to divide the pictures into areas according to their subject matter. Any kind of systematization on the basis of the age at which she executed the drawings has been sacrificed although Nadia's age when each drawing was done is sometimes given. However, in many cases this was ascertained from her mother's memory and accurate dating cannot be given. The selection represents about one quarter of her total available output at September, 1974. They were chosen to show variety and skill. The drawings are arranged in the following categories:

Subject	Nadia's age when subject first appeared	Frequency
Horses	3 years 5 months	Frequent. Her favourite subject
Horse and rider	4 years	Frequent
Cockerel	6 years 4 months	Frequent
Birds	3 years 6 months	Infrequent
Pelican	6 years 5 months	Only 3 or 4 drawings were produced over a one-month period
Dogs	4 years	Infrequent
Other animals		Have occurred from time to time and a few drawings of each were made
Trains	3 years 6 months	Only 5 or 6 drawings exist, spread over 3 years
Human figures	4 years–6 years 6 months	Frequent

The drawings illustrate Nadia's exceptional gifts and their quality is self-evident. However, attention can be drawn to the following points.

Horses are drawn in many orientations. She appears to have as easy a facility in both right and left positions whereas most young children have a preferred orientation (Harris, 1963). The horses vary in size but retain their quality of form. Nadia's earliest drawings, made when she was $3\frac{1}{2}$ years old, are of horses. It is of course most unusual for a child to choose horses as a first subject. Most children first draw humans or houses. Her earliest horses were fun-fair horses—and the details include saddle and bridle with their ornamental trimmings and the central support pole. The round supports on the bridle and bit are clearly drawn. Her attention to detail and portrayal must have outstripped her knowledge of the uses and func-tions of these objects, as she had only seen horses on occasional visits to parks and zoos and had ridden only once at the seaside. Her intimate knowledge of horses was gained from pictures.

There are several drawings showing a horse and rider. The rider is usually a man; the horse appears in both right and left orientation but usually at the same angle to the viewer. These drawings especially illustrate Nadia's use of perspective and foreshortening. The details of the tunic (Drawing 24, p. 33) show epaulettes, buttons on the front and sleeve, and cross straps on the chest and also the satchel. The angles of the box-like satchel are clearly shown. The fingers placed around the trumpet—not only the correct number of fingers—but the fact that the trumpet disappears behind them is remarkable—the normal child has great difficulty in portraying one object behind another and either fails altogether or distorts in the attempt. The details of the horse show a similar observation of detail and mastery of perspective. The angle of the leather bit strap over the nose in Drawing 24 illustrates this.

Also in Drawing 24 there is an indication of the line of the hills. This illustrates Nadia's use of distance and horizon and gives the illusion of the land receding into the distance—a sophisticated device used at a much later stage, normally. In Drawing 30 the horse is gal-loping and rearing. The head is lifted and the mouth is open. There is a boldness and almost an aggressive quality to this picture. At one period her riders were headless.

The next section illustrates a recurring theme which Nadia first began to draw in February 1974. These cockerel drawings show especially well Nadia's ability to change orientation, angle and position. She had very little first-hand experience of chickens, according to her mother, and it is amazing how she could alter the head position and still retain the likeness without experience of the three-dimensional object and the real shape. If one saw a drawing of a ball, for example, it would be hard to tell from the drawing alone whether the shape was flat—like a plate, like a discus, or like a ball. Nadia evidently had a good idea of a three-dimensional object from a two-dimensional representation. We can see this from the many re-orientations of objects which she achieved.

The picture-book cockerel which originally caught Nadia's eye, and which her teacher believed she imitated, is also reproduced (Fig. 4, p. 43). Nadia's Drawing 34 is very like the original in all respects, especially the raised foot and claw. However, this drawing was not copied and was done some weeks after the original had been taken away. The cockerel is also turned more towards the viewer so that more of the interior of the mouth is visible, including the lower interior as indicated by a short but definite extra line. The circle of the eye is also more oblique than the eye of the original. She has shaded the interior of the mouth but has ignored the heavy colour of the stomach feathers in the original. She has recognized the need for shading in the one area where it is most essential.

On several of the cockerel drawings (35–38, 40, 41) Nadia has included a tongue although none exists on the original. As Drawing 43 shows a different kind of chicken Nadia must have seen other chicken pictures and it is possible that she remembered many details so that her drawings are a composite of several images.

In the section of drawings of human figures, Drawings 73 and 74 comprise some of Nadia's earliest drawings drawn when she was approximately 4 years old. A Goodenough Harris "Draw a Woman: Assessment" on number 73 gives Nadia a score of 28 which gives her an IQ score of 160!

We can see from Drawings 82 and 85 that Nadia could draw moving figures in a wide variety of positions with legs and arms raised, and could create an impression of movement. We can see, too, that she used the characteristic "cockerel's eye" on many of her human and animal figures. Children rarely attempt profile or three-quarter view figures at this age as Nadia has done.

I had the opportunity to watch the evolution of Nadia's approach to the final subject in the selection—the legs and shoes (pp. 88–95). All her drawings to September 1974 are included. Each drawing is from a slightly different angle—but all were of high quality from the first attempt. It was evident that Nadia did not need to practise her subject before executing a highly competent drawing. I also noticed that she studied legs and feet attentively once she was interested in the subject, following their movement and staring at people's shoes—occasionally touching them.

Further Experimental Investigation of Nadia's Ability

I knew that Nadia preferred to draw with a ball-point pen or fine felt-tipped pen on white paper of manageable size, but as I continued to work with her I presented her with a variety of different art materials to see if she could exploit her abilities in another medium.

Although I gave her a wide array of coloured felt pens Nadia showed no use of colour—nor was she interested in colouring outlined drawings in a picture book I gave her. She used the coloured pens independently to draw her usual line drawings; the strongest colours red and green were her preference but she never used them together.

I gave Nadia brushes of various sizes and tried both Rowney inks and pre-mixed powder paints. Although Nadia understood their use as she painted at school, she only once attempted to draw a recognizable outline with a brush. When this line smudged, she scribbled and daubed on the paper and soon gave up. When tempted into painting she would daub in this fashion producing an "abstract" typical of a normal 6-year-old child, but treated this medium with evident frustration and would quickly leave it. She would attempt a line drawing in crayon, in one colour, providing the crayon was fine enough, but became frustrated by larger crayons and would only "scrub" up and down, before becoming bored. Similarly, Nadia would attempt a line drawing with a fine pen and ink, but quickly smudged lines previously drawn as she moved her hand over the surface of the paper. She did not understand how this had happened and would discard the drawing once she noticed that it had been spoiled.

I showed Nadia plasticine and Play doh and indicated to her how a model horse could be fashioned in these materials; she watched with attention and interest and played with the materials—but made no attempt to make a recognizable object.

She developed the obsessive habit of cutting paper into small strips less than one-tenth of an inch wide. She showed considerable dexterity with scissors and could cut along lines and shapes that had been drawn for her.

Despite my frequent attempts to interest her in coloured and black and white pictures Nadia did not draw directly from them. It was difficult to tell whether later drawings were inspired by these pictures—certainly no outstanding examples were forthcoming. I also presented to her toy horses and other animals with a white card background so that the image would be distinct. Occasionally a toy horse would cause her to draw a horse—but not the horse in front of her. On the only occasion that I saw Nadia draw from life, when she drew me, she studied my face for several minutes before drawing. She drew quickly and laughed a great deal while working (Drawing 89). On another occasion I drew a duck, copied from a child's picture book (Fig. 6) while Nadia watched with some interest. When I had finished Nadia drew several birds but not the duck that I had drawn, although the picture remained close at hand. (See Drawings 50 and 51.)

If Nadia had possessed eidetic imagery and therefore drew by tracing around the projected outline of a figure which she could see in her mind's eye, then she should have been able to trace around the image of an object seen through a semi-opaque surface. I gave her a black and white outline drawing of a dog covered with tracing paper. I demonstrated a few lines of tracing and Nadia completed the image. Whereas many of the exercises I demonstrated were pointless to her, she evidently understood and gained satisfaction from tracing. The implications of this are discussed more fully on pp. 112–113.

Gestalt theory suggests that adults and children will reduce ambiguities in drawings (Harris, 1963). I gave Nadia some figures which had been traced from her own drawings, but from which the heads had been omitted. She immediately filled in the heads on both the pictures, thus establishing that she perceived her animals as "wholes". This also suggests that when she sometimes drew humans with pinheads (see Drawing 101) it was not an omission of detail, but was deliberate.

Analysis of Drawing by Use of Video-film

A timed, stage by stage breakdown of Nadia's drawing was made possible by the use of videofilm. The film was stopped at appropriate time-intervals and a rough reconstruction of each new line was made on successive pieces of tracing paper placed over the original drawing (see pp. 30–31).

This allowed a close inspection of Nadia's technique. One of the remarkable facts about the drawing of the horse's head as shown, was that Nadia began with its neck. (All Children and most untrained adults begin drawing an animal with the outline of the head.)

Nadia then positioned the ears before drawing the rest of the head so that at one point she achieved the remarkable feat of having related the neck and ears in a correct spatial relationship without guidance from the lines of the head that were still to be drawn. Of all the drawings I examined, this was the only time this particular horse appeared, so we must exclude the possibility that the drawing was so well practised that she could start at any point.

Some of the drawings have been extremely difficult to reproduce. In a small proportion of cases only photocopies of the originals were available. These photocopies have been reproduced despite their poorer quality. Another problem has been that Nadia drew on whatever paper was to hand, including reading books, lined exercise books and even paper cartons. All the drawings have been reproduced at their original size.

2

Four horses. Note details of saddles, bridles etc. and fairground poles in 1 and 4. These horses were some of Nadia's earliest drawings, drawn from the age of 3 years 5 months. Numbers 1–14 were all drawn before she was 4 years of age.

3

4

6

8

10

11

If drawing number 13 is turned to the right another horse is visible. Drawn at approximately 3 years 5 months.

13

A similar group of horses as in Drawing 13, but note the dog to the right of centre, and the rider on the centre horse. Drawn at approximately 3 years 5 months.

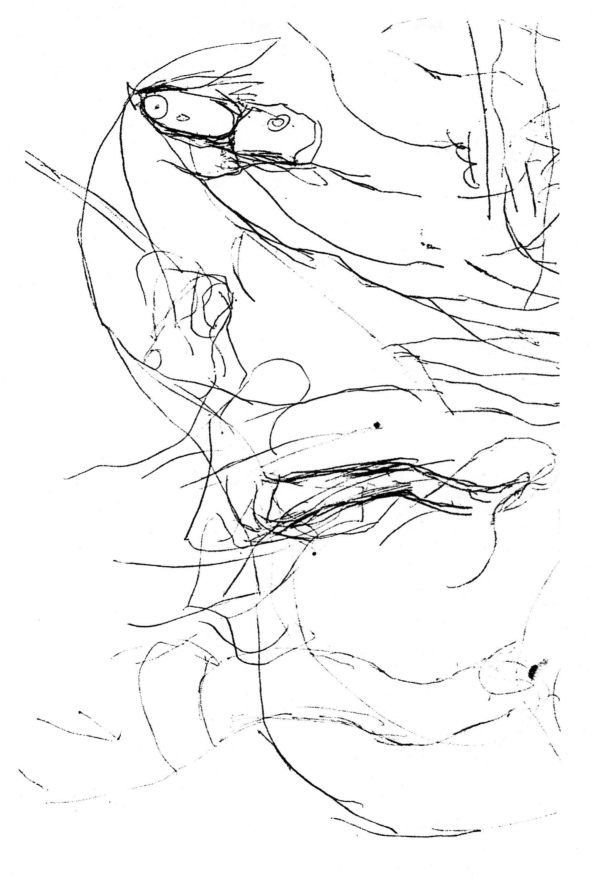

Drawings 15–19 show six horses heads and give a good selection of Nadia's ability to experiment with angle and orientation and to vary the expression of the horse. This group were all drawn at approximately 5 years.

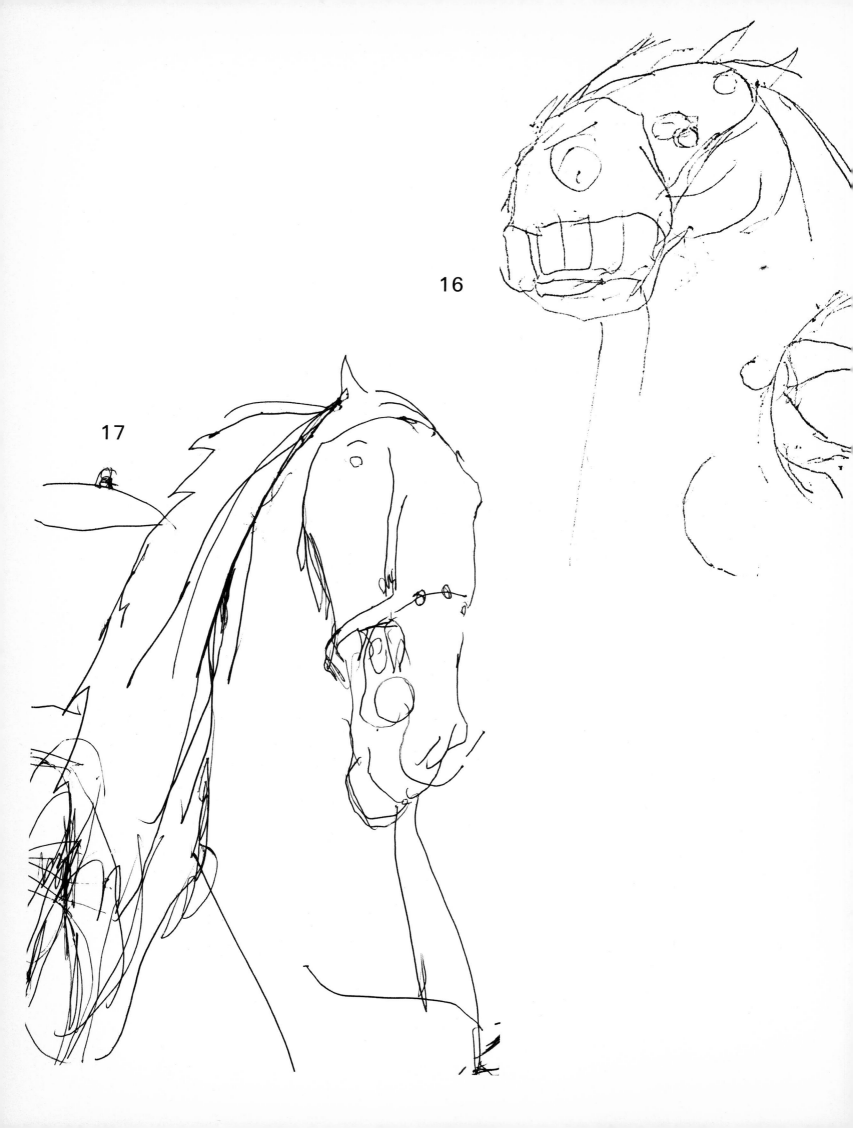

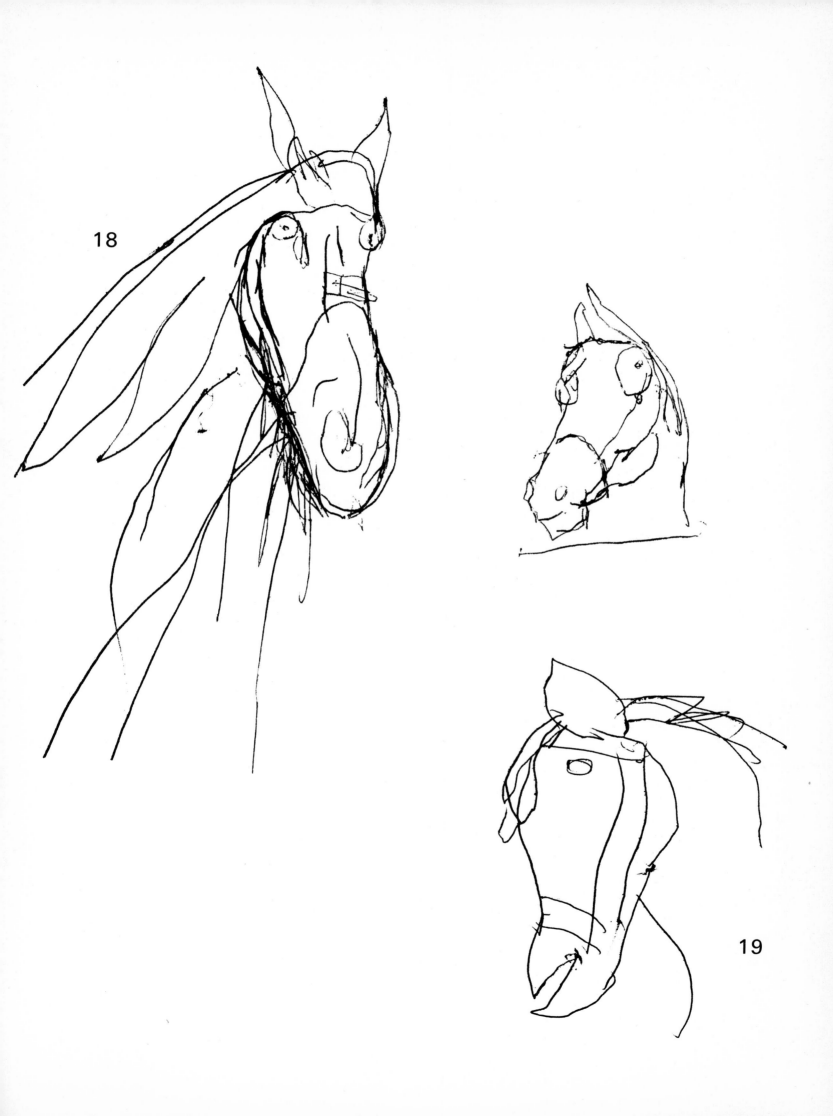

20

Two fine examples of movement. Horse number 21 is an
early drawing, at approximately 4 years.

21

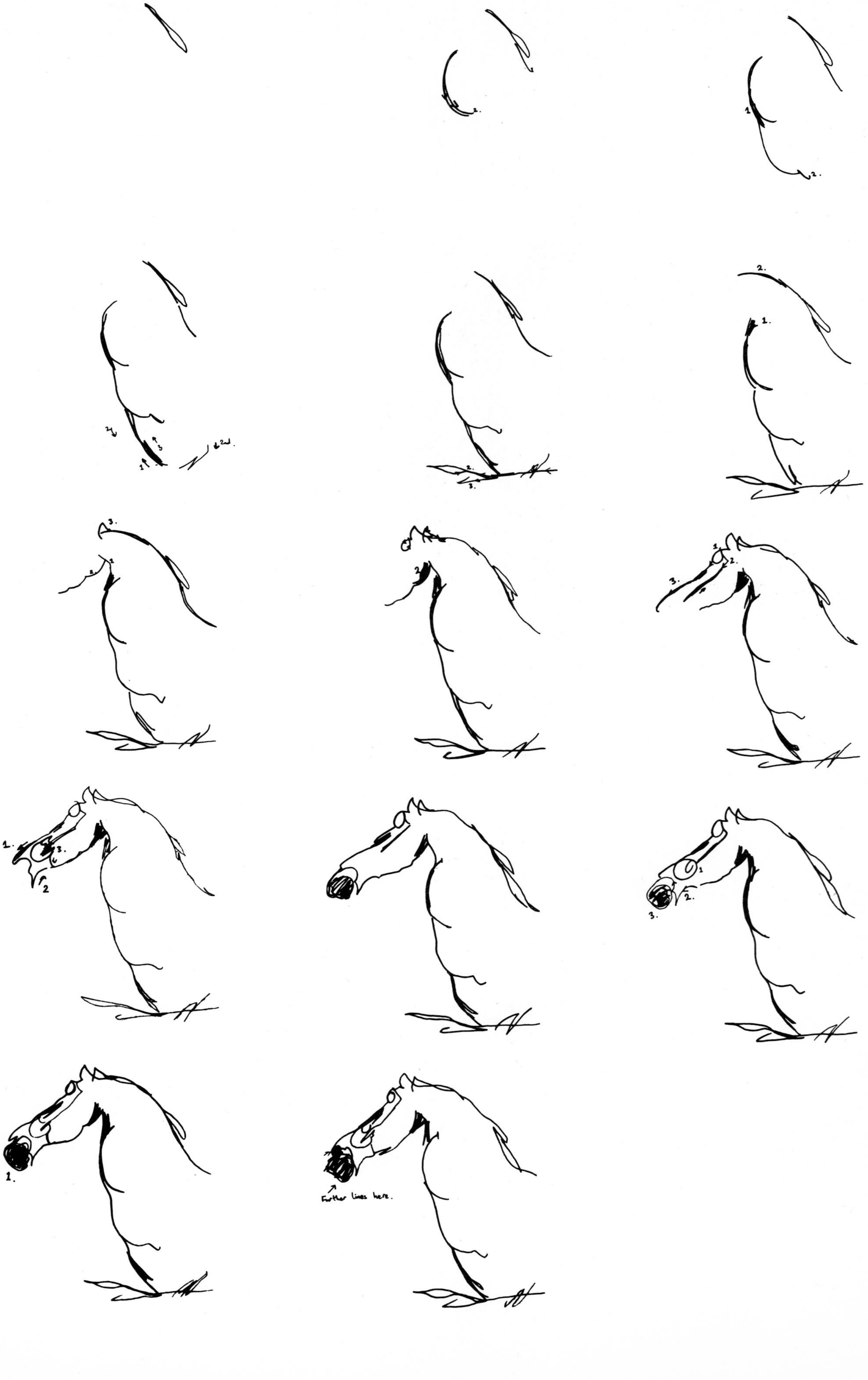
Further lines here.

Fig. 1

Fig. 1 shows the completed drawing. A line by line reconstruction of this drawing made with the aid of a video-tape is shown on p. 30 (right to left and top to bottom). The drawing took approximately two minutes to complete.

22

23

Drawings 22–32 show a range of Nad favourite subject—horse and rider. The drawings (number 23) appeared when she 4 years.

24

This drawing is very detailed. Note the bridle, tunic, trumpet and hand, together with the inappropriate and disturbing face, and squirrel on the horse's side. Drawn at approximately 5 years 6 months.

Nadia is equally able at right or left portrayal.

26

Again, we have the same rider shown in left and right orientations. Note the details of the hand holding trumpet. Drawn at approximately 5 years.

28

2

30

31

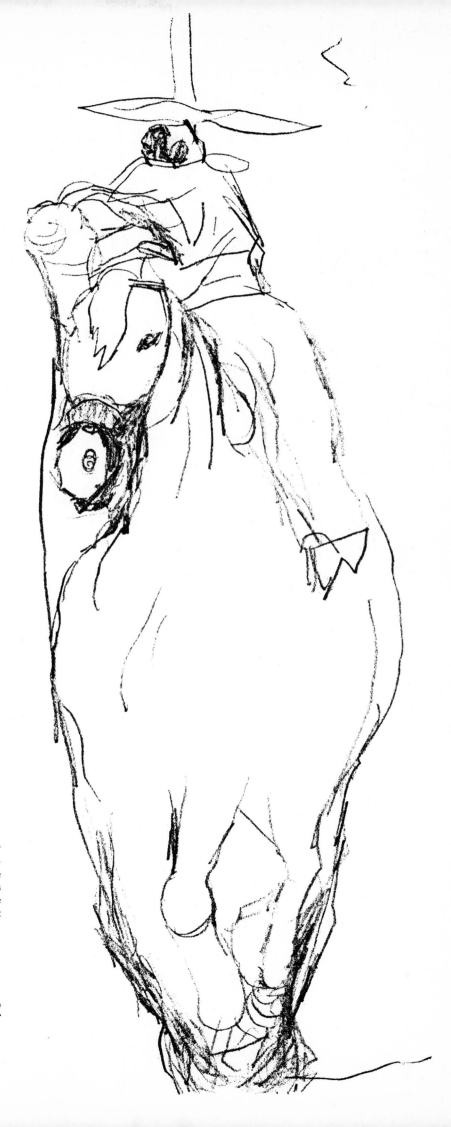

The two soldiers seen in numbers 29–32 are completely different from the rider with trumpet in previous drawings. They seem to be crusaders on chargers Note the sword seen clearly in 31. The head of the horse in 32 is drawn with great sensitivity and the angle at which the horse jumps out of the page would tax the skills of most skilled artists. Drawn at approximately 5 years.

32

Fig. 2

Figs 2 and 3 show examples of Nadia's source of inspiration. Her only experience of horses was from pictures such as these. It must be emphasized, however, that she did *not* copy the pictures and drew without them being present. Reproduced with permission from Ladybird Books Ltd., Loughborough.

Here comes Wait-For-Me, at last.
And oh!
Here comes the great big rooster!

Fig. 4

This cockerel from Nadia's picture book introduces the second main group of drawings.

33

Nadia has begun a second rooster at the bottom of this drawing, and upside down. Occasionally, a line in one drawing would suggest another subject to her and two drawings would appear —one on top of the other.

34

This drawing is very close to its original. Note the stray breast feathers and the lifted leg. All Nadia's cockerel drawings on these and the following pages were drawn at approximately 6 years 4 months.

35

36

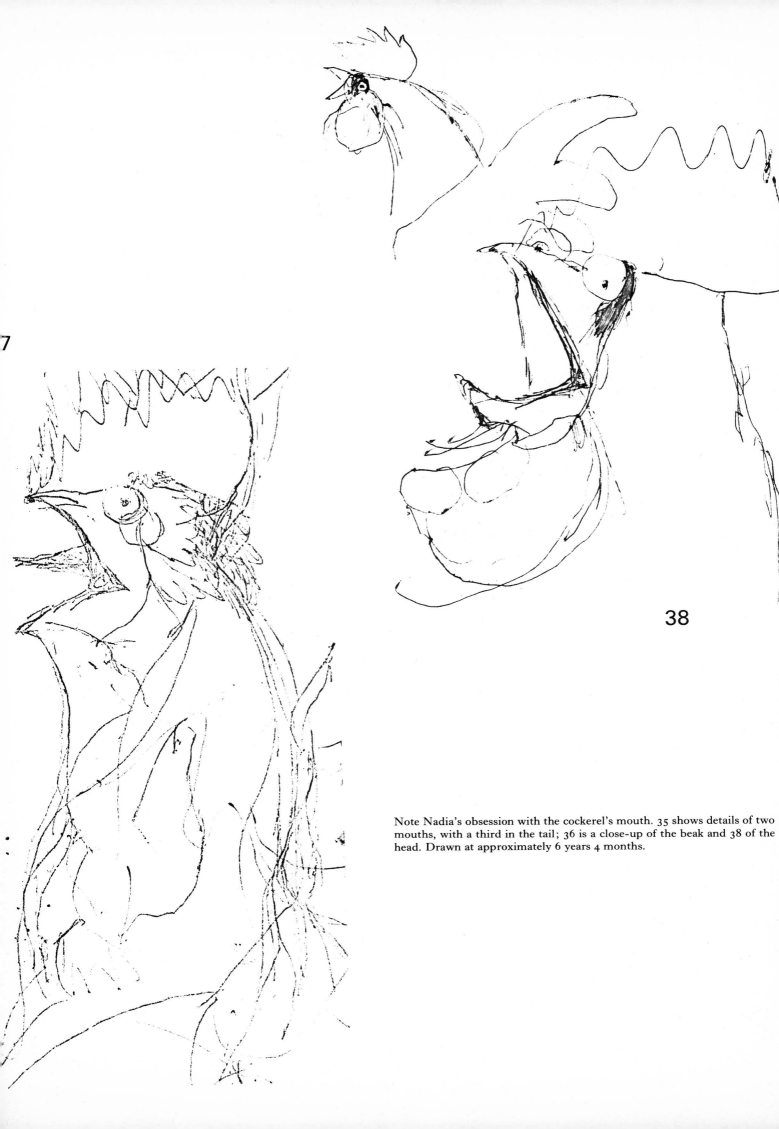

37

38

Note Nadia's obsession with the cockerel's mouth. 35 shows details of two mouths, with a third in the tail; 36 is a close-up of the beak and 38 of the head. Drawn at approximately 6 years 4 months.

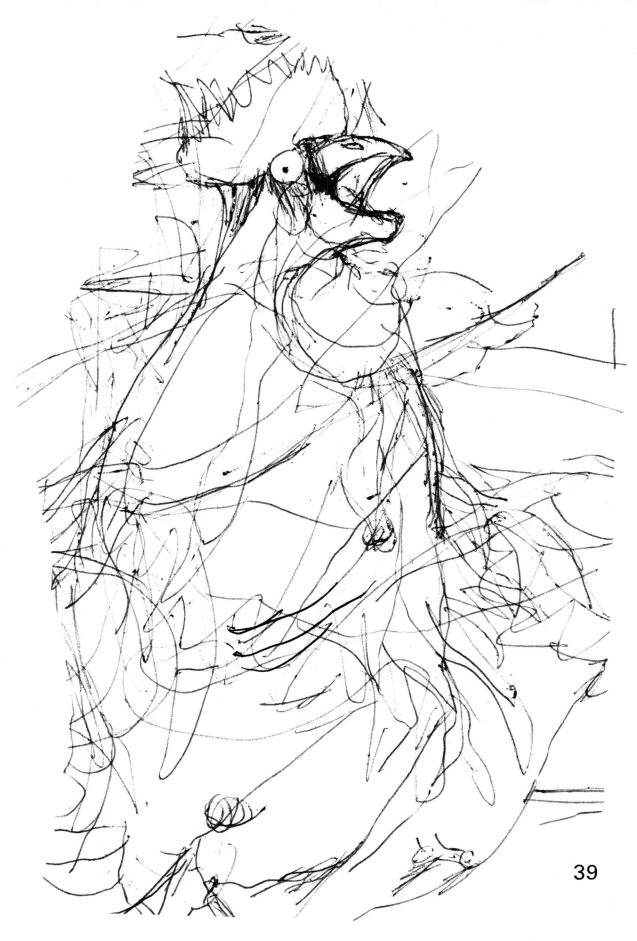

39

Three more cockerels with open mouths and tongues—a feature not included in the picture book cockerel (Fig. 4). Drawn at approximately 6 years 4 months. Again, Nadia is able to alter the angle of the head and appropriately adjust the amount of the interior of the mouth that would be visible.

40

41

43

44

Drawing 42 shows a cockerel, with a chicken on right; 43 is another "chicken" (note horse's head appearing on left), while 44 is a garden bird on a branch. These are some of Nadia's earliest drawings at approximately 3 years 6 months.

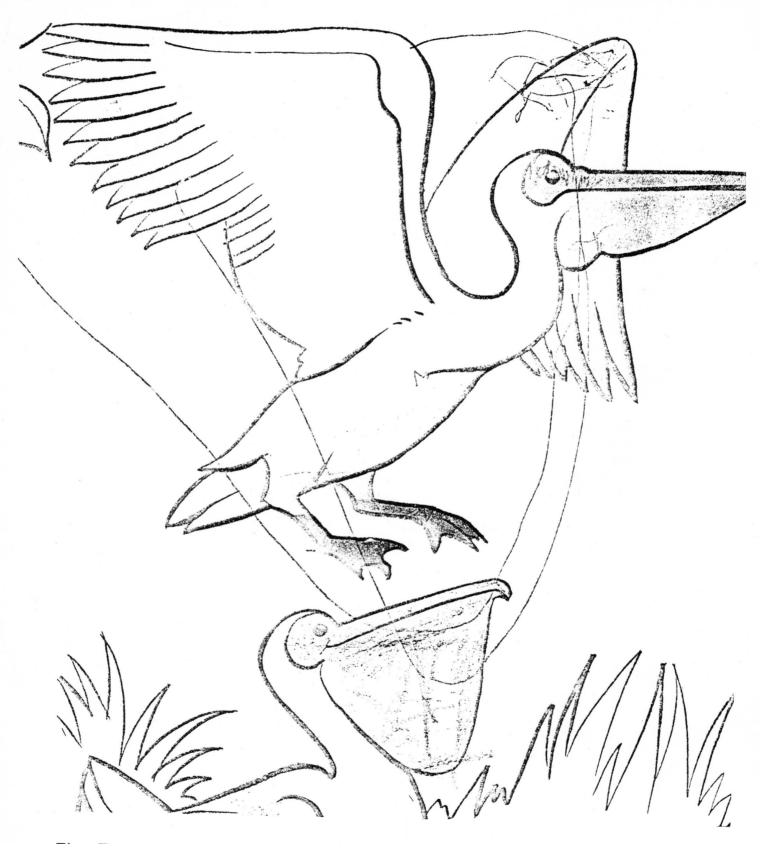

Fig. 5

This print of two pelicans introduces the section of Nadia's pelican drawings, although the print was not available when she drew her birds. Note also the inclusion faithfully of the second head at the foot of the page. All pelican drawings drawn at approximately 6 years 5 months. Three-quarters of Nadia's total output of pelicans are included here. This underlines the fact that she did not need to practise to perfect the drawings.

45

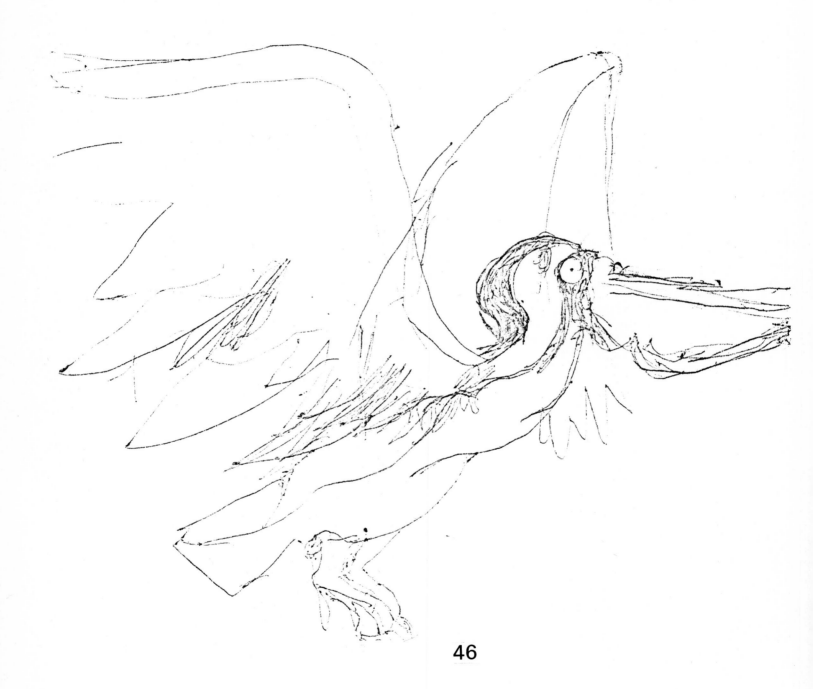

46

47

48

This is another example of Nadia's strange ability to reproduce minor details without access to the original. Detail from lower half of Drawing number 46. Drawn at 6 years 7 months.

A typical example of one of Nadia's composite drawings—including all subjects so far examined. Note horse at left and cat at lower left (see Fig. 4) also cockerel with open mouth and tongue. Drawn at approximately 6 years 3 months.

49

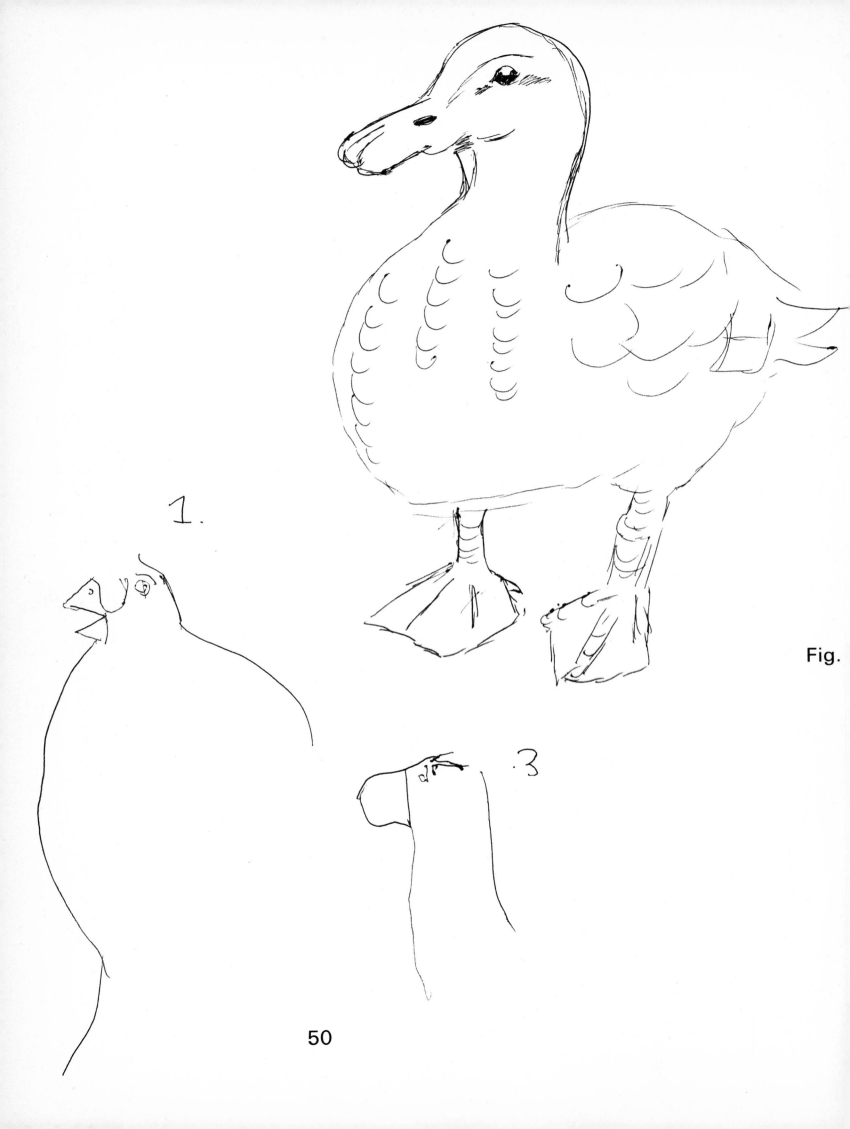

1.

.3

Fig.

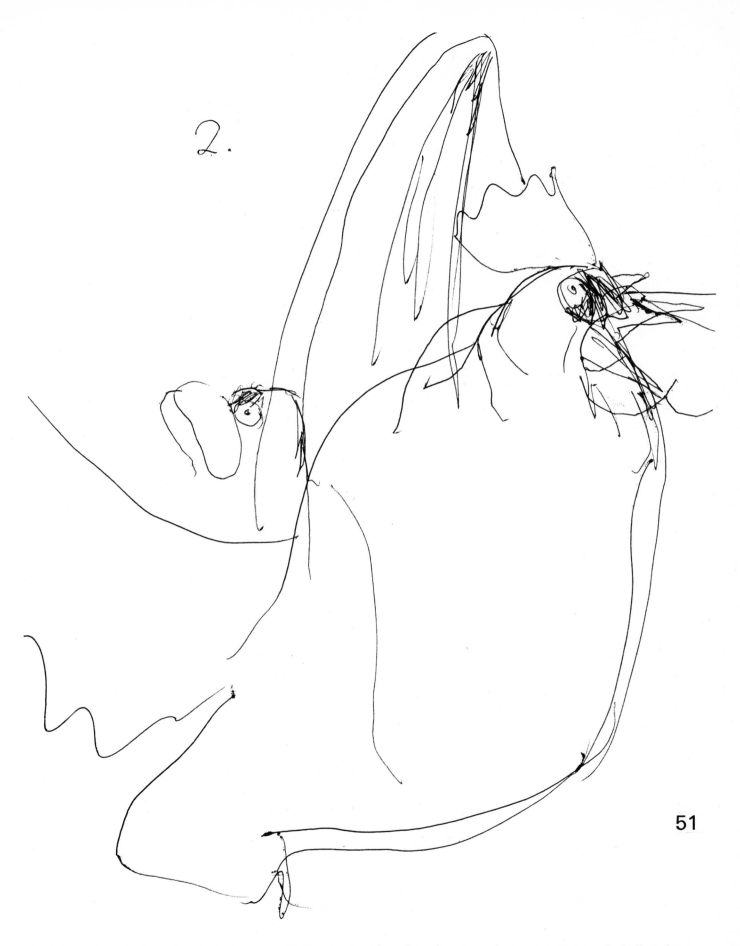

2.

51

Fig. 6 shows the author's version of a duck given to Nadia to inspire her to draw. Her attempts (50 and 51) in the order indicated are interesting as they are not of the same quality as her usual drawings but she abandoned the drawing above (51) to turn it into her cockerel—showing that she recognized that the duck and cockerel were both birds. Drawn at approximately 6 years 6 months.

52

Dogs and cats. Note that 53 (detail from 49) is inspired by Fig. 4. Drawn at approximately 4 years except for 53 drawn at approximately 6 years 3 months.

53

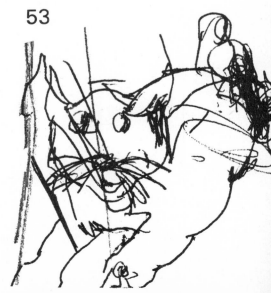

54

55

57

Drawing 57 shows a rather more menacing dog than those seen so far.

58

59

Drawing 58 is an example of how Nadia could scribble on a drawing, perhaps if she was dissatisfied with it. Drawing 59 shows the same subject. Drawn at approximately 4 years.

A LADYBIRD

Fifth Picture Book

by ETHEL and HARRY WINGFIELD

The Ladybird Picture Books are ideally suited for use with the Ladybird 'Under Five' series 'Learning with Mother' and its associated Playbooks.

Publishers: Ladybird Books Ltd . Loughborough
© Ladybird Books Ltd 1973
Printed in England

Fig. 7

Fig. 7 shows a page from one of Nadia's picture books. Nadia often scribbled over the lines in books, selecting only certain areas that caught her attention (note the mane, muzzle and tail). She has drawn her version on the book (left). Reproduced with permission from Ladybird Books Ltd., Loughborough.

60

Two lions lie side by side but when the page is turned to right a reverse image of the dog in Drawing 55 appears. Nadia often seemed to be inspired by the shape of a part of a finished drawing to then turn it into a different drawing. The animals in this group were drawn from when Nadia was 4 years old to when she was approximately 6 years old. Only a few drawings of each animal were made.

61

A strange composite animal, part giraffe—part donkey.

62

A reindeer, drawn in January 1974, probably inspired by a Christmas picture. Nadia was 6 years 3 months at this time.

64

63

63 and 64 show simple drawings of a cat and a giraffe. 65 is rather more complex. We see the giraffe with detailed neck markings; the rough lines to the right of the drawing imply the movement of the neck as the animal bends to eat.

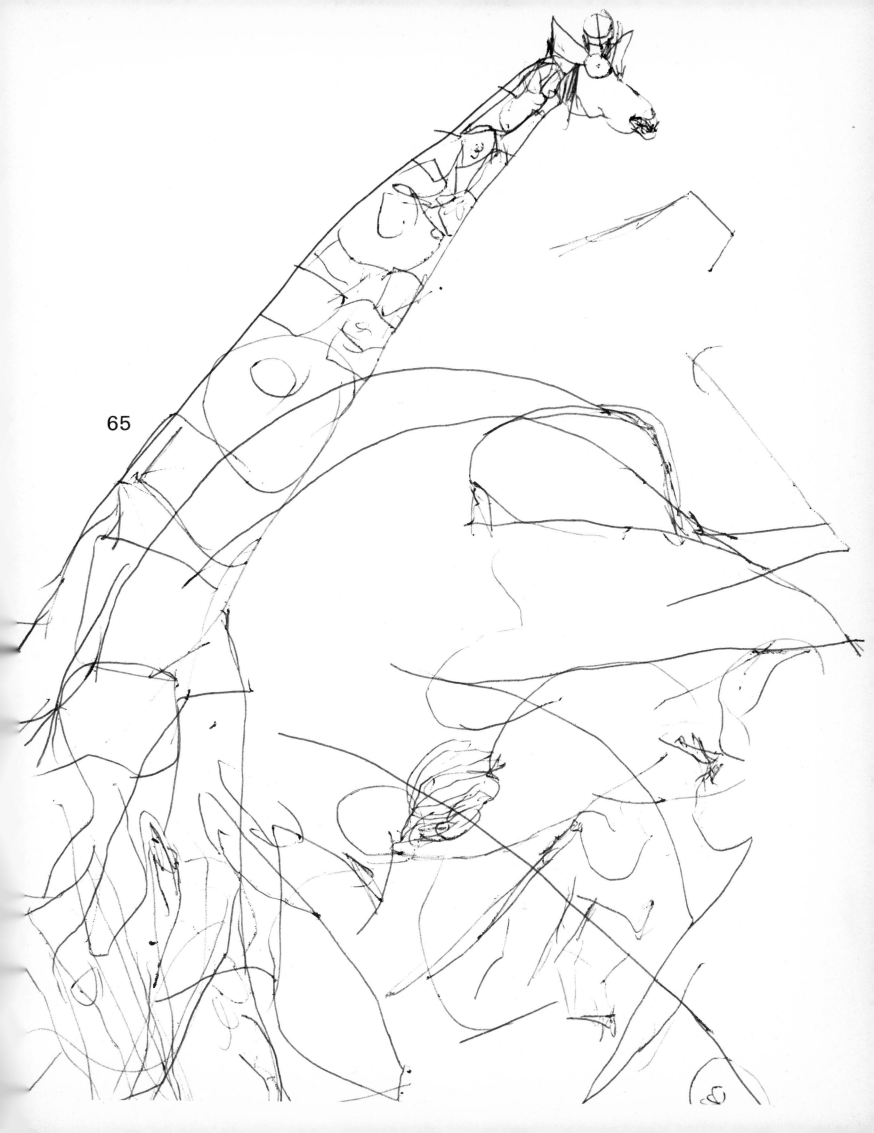

65

66

A beautiful elephant's head turned to the left. (Nadia's drawing in pale pink crayon was difficult to reproduce.)

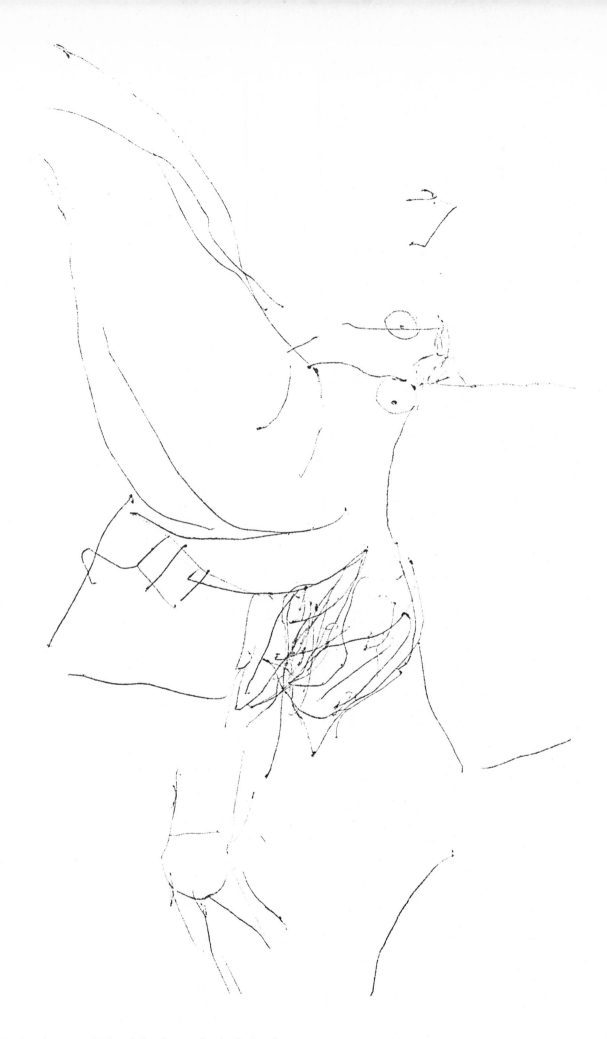

67

This drawing shows an elephant's head—trunk raised, mouth open.

68

70

69

These early drawings almost make up a farmyard scene; 68 shows a cow, horse's head and pig or cow (lower left); 69 and 70 again show pigs and a cow.

One of Nadia's earliest drawings—of a train. We can also see, if the page is turned, three animal heads. Drawn at approximately 3 years 6 months.

71

72

73

74

The train in 72 is one of Nadia's earliest drawings (approximately 3 year
6 months). 73 and 74 show early, human figures. Drawn at approximately
4 years.

The familiar horse and rider is on the left. A human figure on the right. Drawn at approximately 4 years. Her early drawings of the human figure include details of the face. Later drawings show less detail and the circular eye with a dot in the middle predominates.

76

77

78

sibly footballers. Note the strange eye. In 76 the drawing can be turned to show a second
ure. In 77 the repeated outlines of the feet in different positions give a great impression of
vement—rather like the giraffe's neck in 65. Drawn at approximately 5 years.

80

81

Drawing 81 is of a lady on horseback. Note the flounces on her skirt and plumes on her hat. Nadia's lack of materials did not deter her. Number 82 is drawn over a newspaper cutting. Drawn at approximately 4 years.

82

83

This drawing seems, by the helmet and rope, to have been inspired by a deep-sea diver—but closely resembles the figure in 85. Drawn at approximately 4 years.

84

85

The powerful movement of these figures drawn together gives a vivid impression of action. Drawn at approximately 5 years. Note the experimentation with legs in the top left-hand corner.

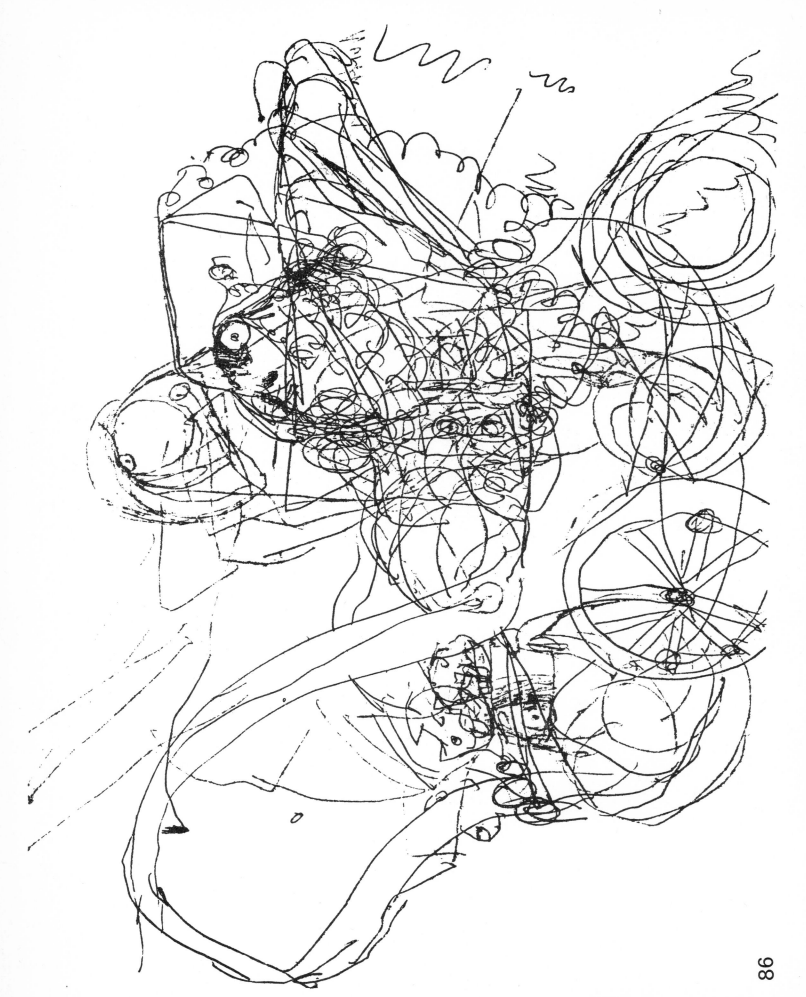

Nadia's impressive drawing of a baby in a pram. Note the cat's head at the foot of the pram. The four circular wheels are of interest. Is she drawing

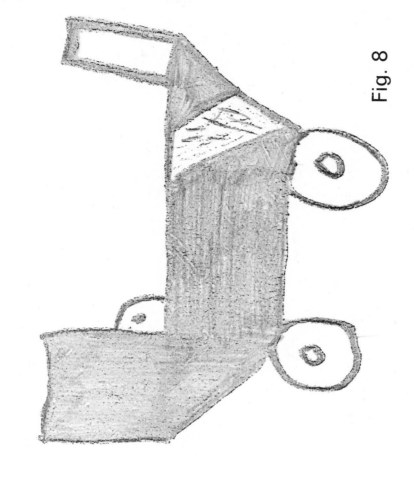

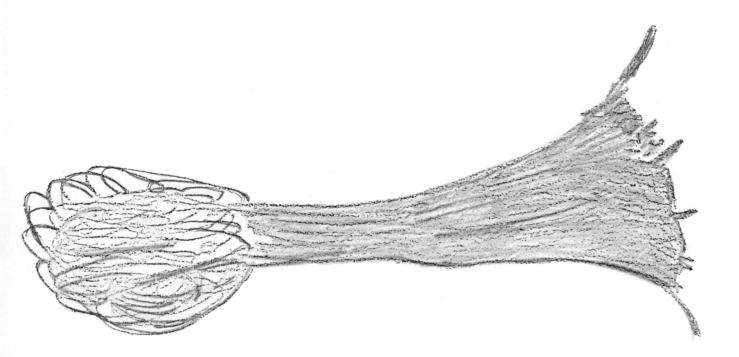

Fig. 8. The contrast with the drawing by a normal 6-year-old of a baby in a pram comes as a complete shock after seeing Nadia's drawing.

Fig. 8

87

Four faces. 89 is Nadia's drawing of the author, from life. Drawn at 6 years 8 months.

88

89

90

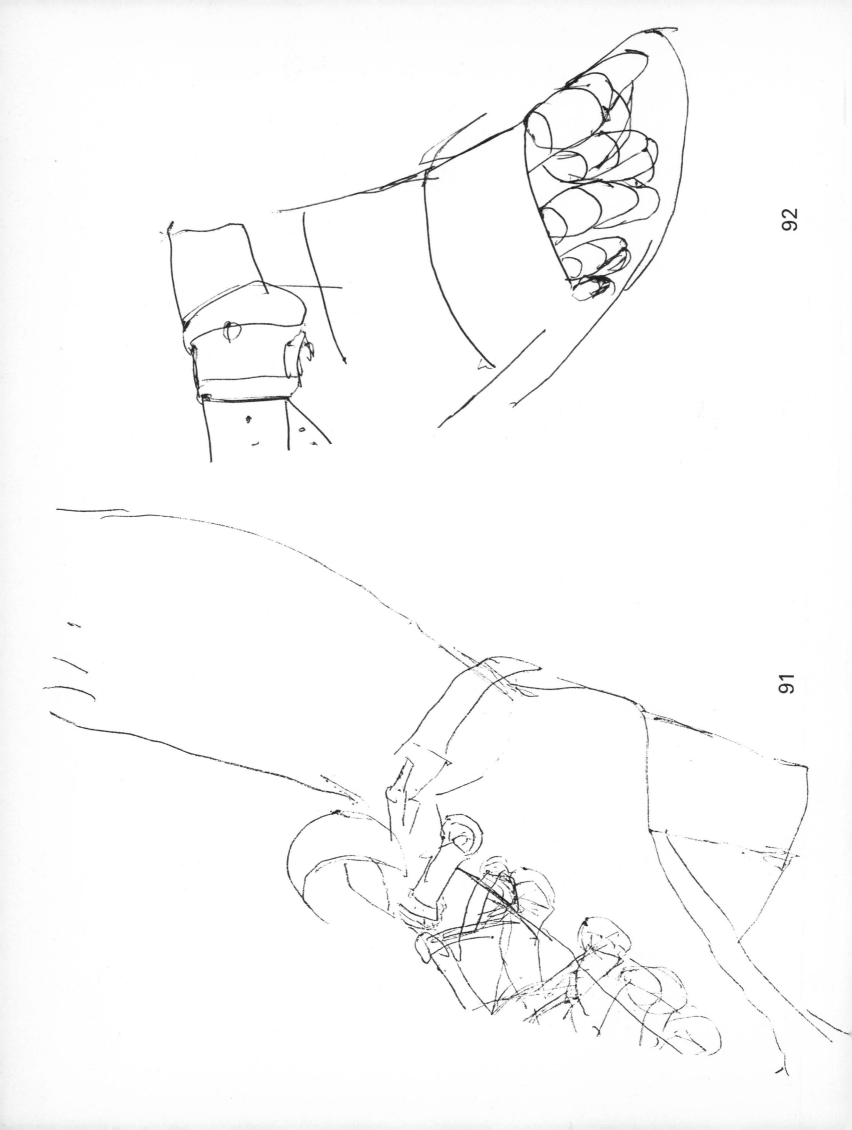

92

91

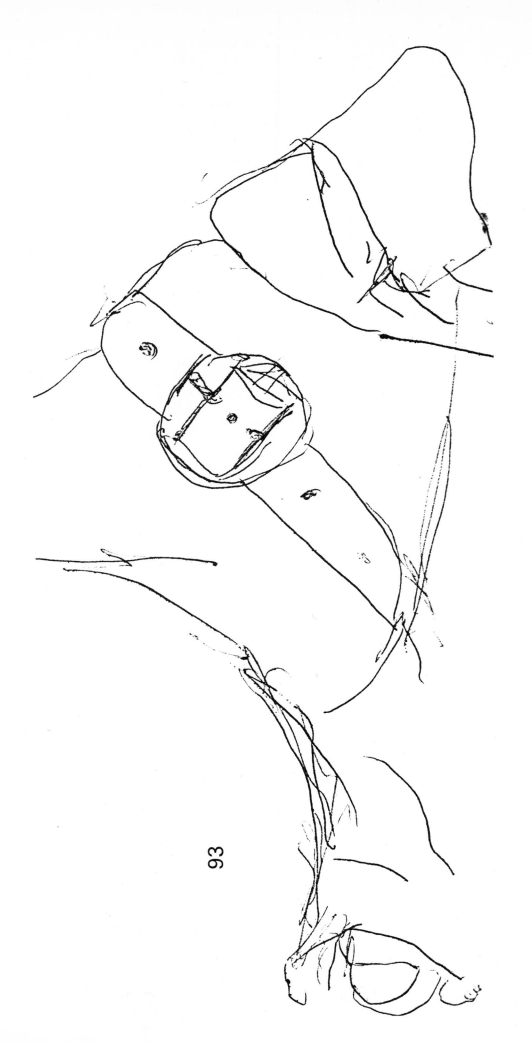

93

Three large studies of feet and shoes, 93 is a side-view of foot in an open sandal, with strap. Drawn at approximately 6 years 8 months.

Four sophisticated studies of crossed legs. Note, too, the detail, as in 96, of the foot balancing a slipper. These and the following drawings of legs and feet were done when Nadia was approximately 6 years 8 months.

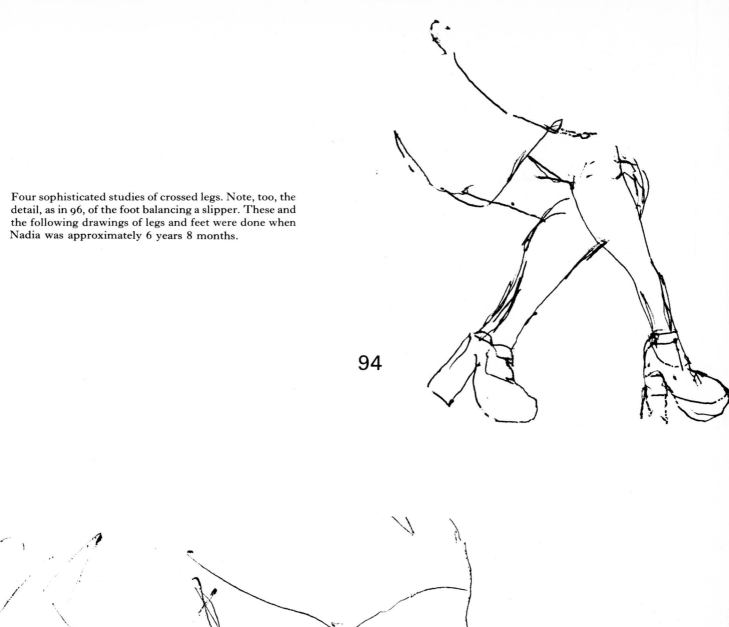

94

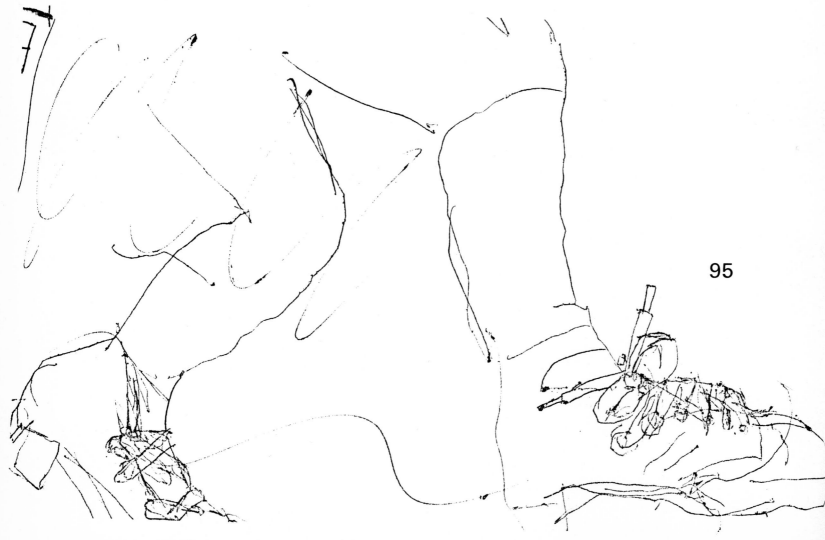

95

96

97

98

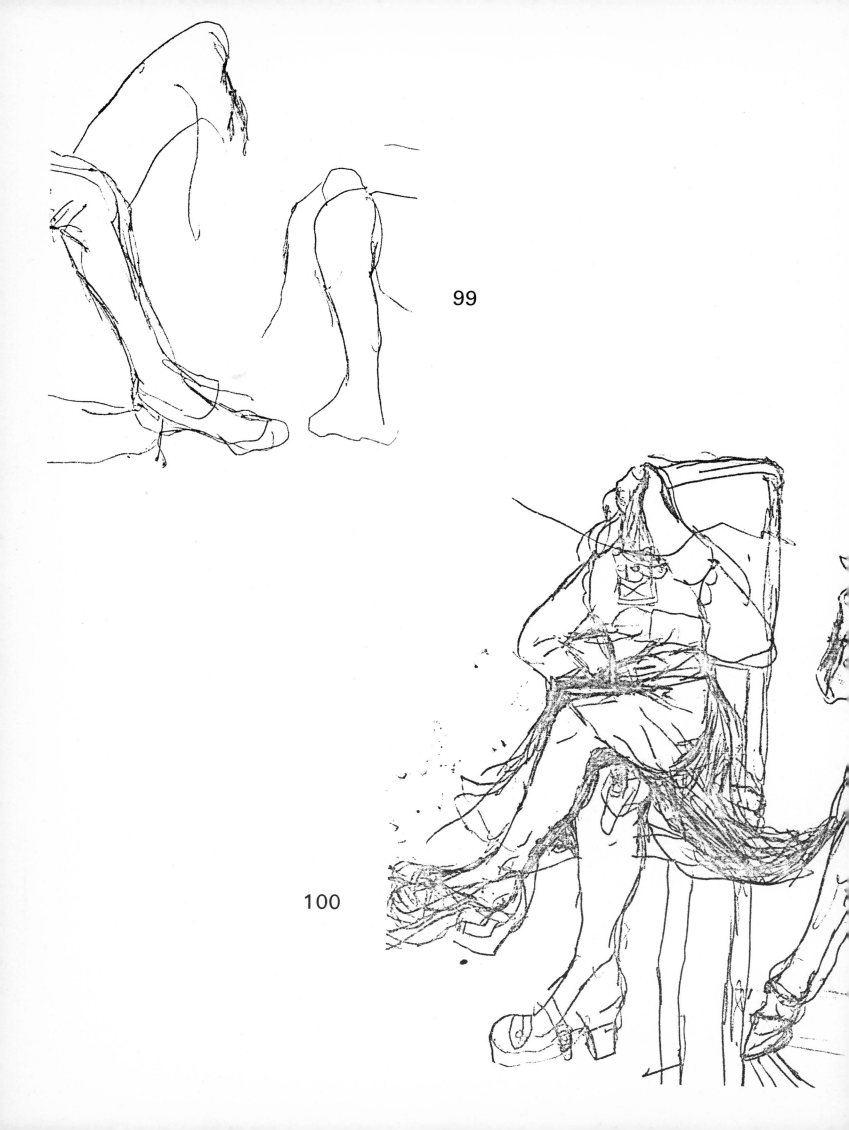

99

100

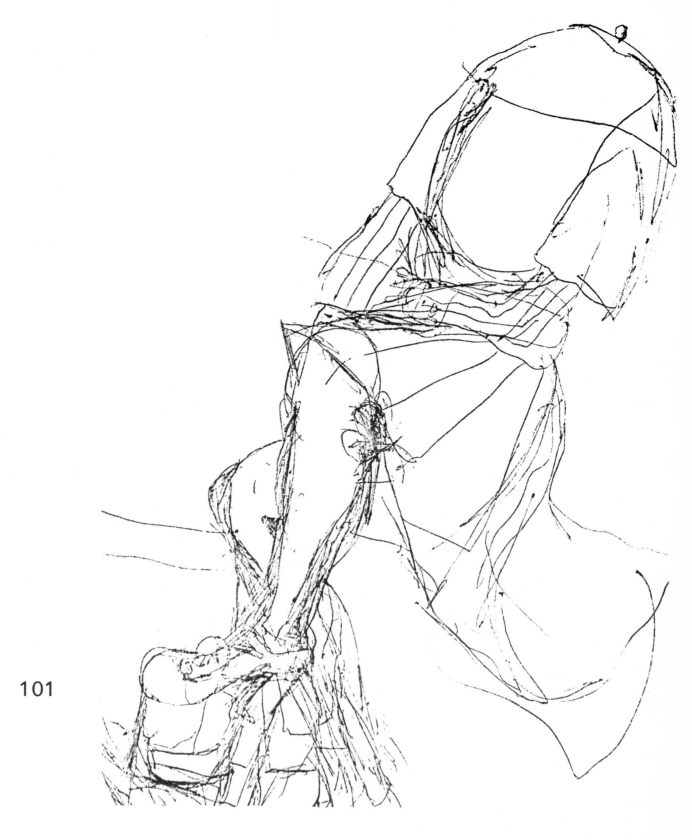

101

Drawings 100 and 101 show similar studies although the details of the shoes are completely different. Drawing 101 is an example of Nadia's pinhead figures. Drawn at approximately 6 years 8 months.

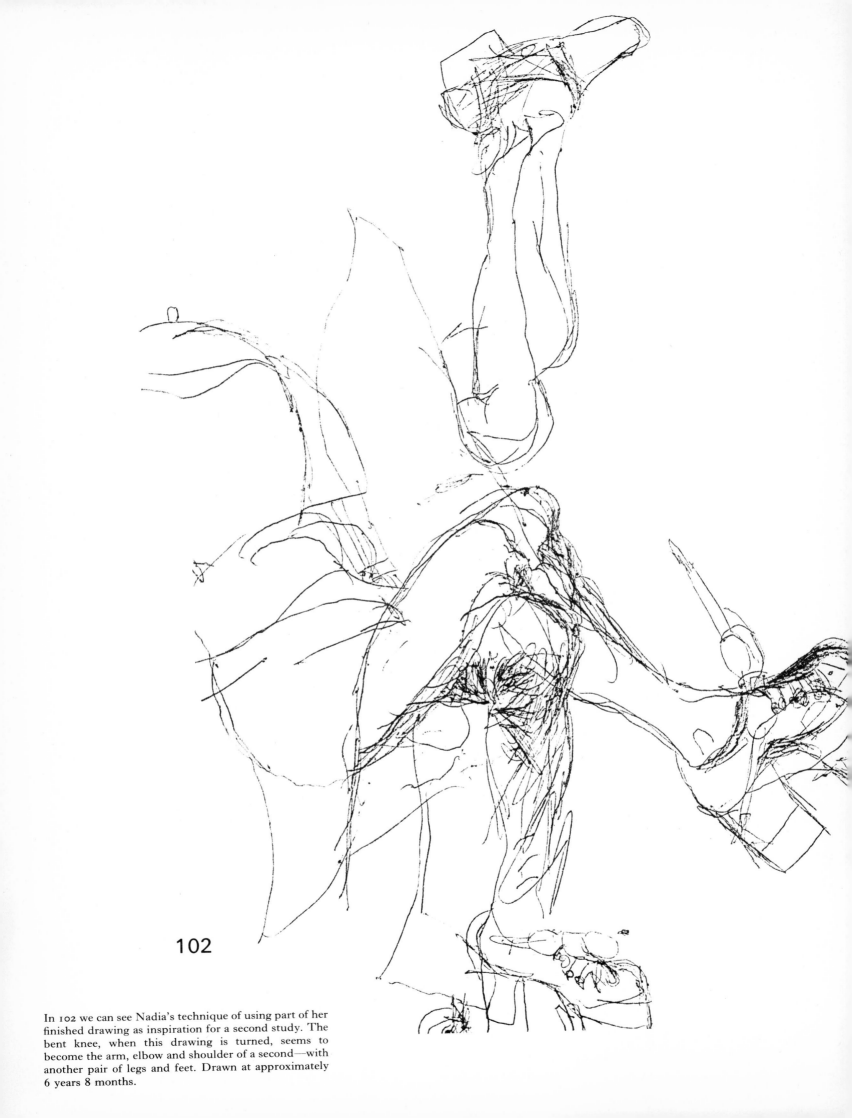

102

In 102 we can see Nadia's technique of using part of her finished drawing as inspiration for a second study. The bent knee, when this drawing is turned, seems to become the arm, elbow and shoulder of a second—with another pair of legs and feet. Drawn at approximately 6 years 8 months.

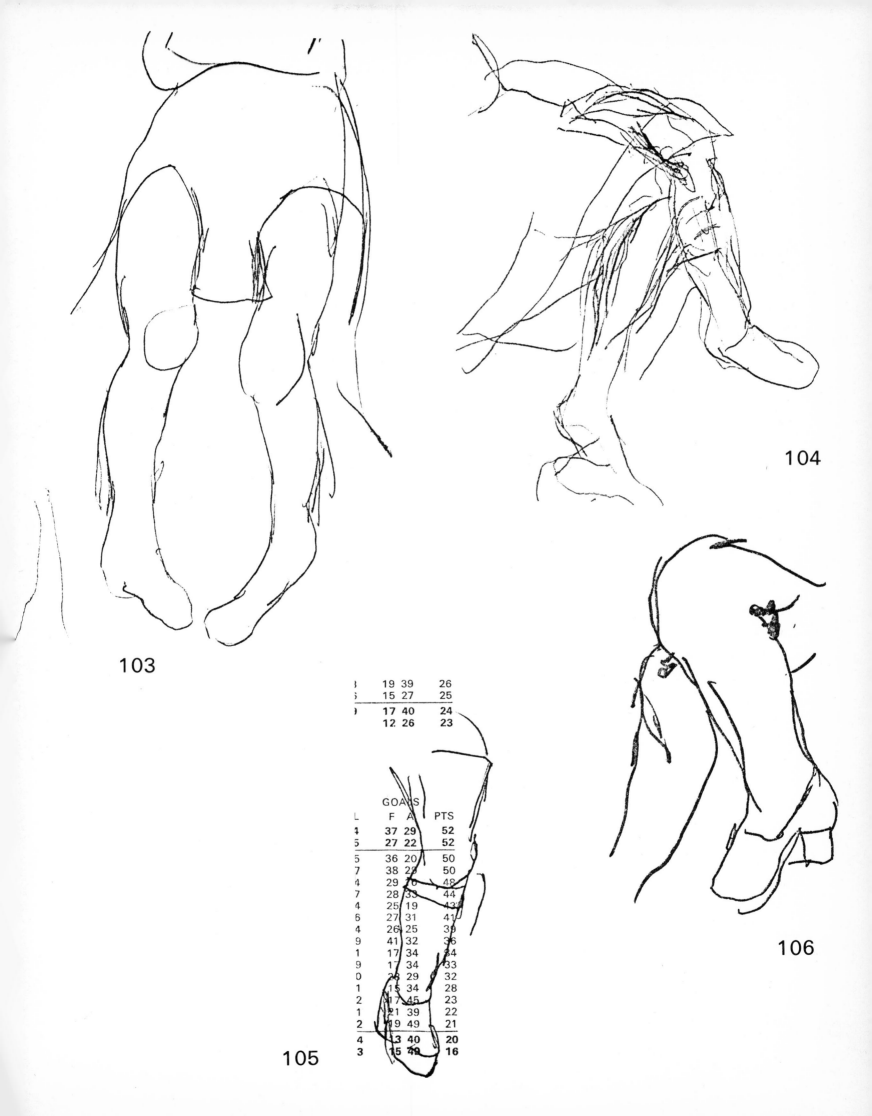

103

104

105

106

In complete contrast to Nadia's work, Figs 9 and 10 show how the average 6-year-old draws a man on a horse.

Figs 11 and 12 show how a 6 to 7-year-old draws a cockerel and a pelican.

Fig. 9

Fig. 10

Fig. 11

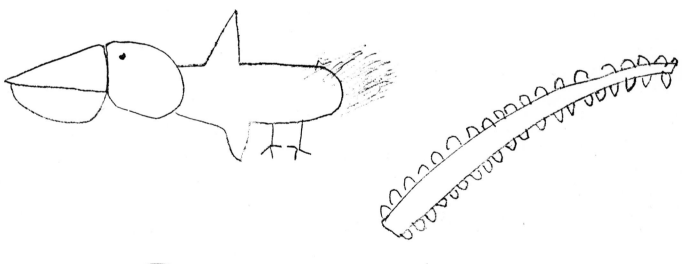

Fig. 12

4

Comparisons

A Comparison of Nadia's Ability with Established Empirical Findings

Before a more general discussion of the theoretical issues can take place, it is important to define some of the terms which are used in this book and to acknowledge and attempt to justify some of the basic assumptions which are made.

Throughout, there is an implied value judgement that one of the important aims of drawing is to be able to reproduce the appearance of the real world. The more faithfully the visual world is represented, the more realistic the drawing, the better it is. It is my contention that, in this respect, Nadia shows a skill far greater than normal children.

This assumption is shared by many psychologists who study children's art. For example, the use of perspective, foreshortening and proportion are always stated to be a "development". It is also shared by some artists and art historians. In our culture, "development" in drawing is viewed as from the use of symbols to a representation of reality. However, it is recognized that an accurate representation of the real world, of the appearance of things, is only one aim in drawing and only one aspect of skill in art. Drawing is also significant as an activity in which children draw their concepts as symbols; in which they express what they know rather than what they see. It is also significant as a means of expressing emotion. In these respects Nadia's drawing is totally anomolous.

It is useful to define some of the concepts used by psychologists, but an outline must of necessity be cursory and is only intended for clarification and to avoid the confusions which arise when general terms differ in their meaning according to different authors. I have defined the terms as flexibly and broadly as possible so that they are not at variance with the views of the major writers in this field, Piaget, Bryant, Bruner and Vygotsky, and I have attempted to interpret theories according to these definitions.

The term "perception" is loosely interpreted to mean the immediate apprehension of the world through the senses. In this book we are almost exclusively concerned with visual perception. Perception is conceived here as the basic registration and reception of visual stimuli. It is useful to attempt to distinguish between reception and interpretation; between seeing and organizing perception, especially because Nadia was such a unique example of receiving and registering information without appearing to understand it. However it is arguably a forced dichotomy, and begs many philosophical questions.

I have used the terms "concept" and "conception" to mean a mental model, abstraction or internal representation of a thing or event in the real world. This is assumed to be the result of a process of organizing sensory input and can be regarded as a higher-order process than perception as it involves memory and processes of discrimination and generalization. The neonate regularly perceives his mother; arising from his regular contact, memory, expectations and innate predispositions he develops a concept of "comforter" and later "mother".

Symbols derive from the conceptualization of reality. They are the realizations of our concepts as spoken words, drawings, signs or writing. In the developing child conceptualization is embodied in visual images as symbols and later in linguistic symbols, as words. Many writers, notably Piaget, emphasize that the symbols do not necessarily bear resemblance to what they symbolize—hence a child's first drawing of a man is often not recognizable as such although the child is satisfied with the result.

In 1926 Goodenough presented a long case and considerable evidence for the view that a child's intelligence can be gauged from his drawing ability and she developed a "Draw-a-Man" measure of intellectual maturity as a result.

Harris (1963) reviewed Goodenough's evidence and brought it up to date and he too, developed the hypothesis that the child's drawing of any object reveals the development of the discriminations and generalizations he has made about that object. He believes that the child's drawing reveals the degree to which his development of a concept of that object as a member of a class has proceeded. The child's drawing of a human being, as a frequently experienced object, becomes a useful index of the growing complexity of his concepts generally.

Recently this position has been heavily criticized by Freeman (1976) who points out that no distinction is offered here between the child's performance and his competence. Harris's work (1963) nevertheless remains the standard text on children's drawing ability and I have therefore, used it extensively to compare and contrast Nadia's ability (pp. 102–107).

The point should be made at the outset of this discussion that although the case of Nadia appears to contradict much of what Harris has to say, experimental studies in psychology give probabilistic or statistical laws which allow for exceptions. Nadia's language deficit and her compensatory development in the field of drawing appear to be unique. However, any theory or general law proposed by Goodenough and Harris which they claim is universal must also allow at least for the possibility of a child like Nadia. The position can be summarized as follows:

1. Where statements of probability are made Nadia's case is not at variance;
2. Where theories are expounded with regard to normal child development Nadia's case is not at variance.
3. Where statements are made which claim to be universal and definitely state that such a case is impossible, Nadia's case is at variance.

Comparison with the Drawing Ability of Normal Children

It is obvious from an examination of Nadia's drawings that her ability is not confined to a few highly practised images executed in a stereotyped manner. It must also be obvious that the normal child of Nadia's age does not draw like this. Elizabeth Newson has summarized the development of children's drawing of the human form as follows:

Stage I : Faces and Cephalopods

Before the age of 2 years, attempts at representation are rare; the child takes pleasure in making simple marks on paper, and in fact produces progressively more sophisticated scribble. Almost invariably the first real picture shows a "face": eyes, nose and mouth in a circle, to which are soon added radiating lines to indicate hair, arms, legs and even fingers. Ears may be drawn within the enclosing circle or totally detached. Orientation is somewhat arbitrary, and the whole drawing may be done upside down. Heads with legs (cephalopods) are comparatively common up to the age of five years. Age range: 2–5 years.

Stage II : Heads, Bodies and Legs

This stage is marked by the introduction of a torso between the head and the legs. The neck is still non-existent, and arms tend to be attached half-way down the body. Hands may be added, often generously supplied with fingers, since at 3–4 years number concepts are limited to "one—two—a lot". Navels, nipples and genitals are often prominent until the child finds that they are socially unacceptable. Variety in colour is still voluntarily restrained. Age range: 3–5 years.

Stage III : Significant Details

The body is elongated and may be given a waist, though this may be hidden by a triangular shift dress. Attachment of arms moves towards shoulder height. Legs remain parallel and set well apart. Both arms and legs begin to have solidity, but tapering towards hands and feet is rare. Accessory details now appear: buttons, pockets, a flower motif on the dress. Hats, shoes, bags etc. may be coloured individually. Age: 4 plus.

Stage IV : Pattern and Decoration

The neck now appears, together with finer details such as pupils, eyebrows and eyelashes. Hair styles and hat designs become more varied, and the legs may move a little closer together. A more definite effort is made to create an interesting "picture": the child exploits pattern, decoration and a range of bright colours with the conscious aim of producing a pleasing overall effect. Age: 5 plus.

Stage V : Static Harmony

Having mastered the basic schema of the human body, together with the problem of dress, the child now turns his attention to filling the background—either by simple colouring, or by the indication of contexts or the addition of subsidiary objects. "Mummy" now becomes "Mummy in the kitchen" or "Mummy in the garden". Figures may be posed against beautiful and complicated backdrops, but they remain essentially static and doll-like. Concepts of perspective are now discernible, but are still extremely primitive. Age: 6 plus.

Stage VI : Dynamic Disruption

The critical stage in child art seems to be reached when the child tries to relate the central figure to its environment by showing Mummy actually engaged in some activity. The harmony of formal arrangement is broken, and problems arise which cannot be solved by the use of decoration and colour. People in action need to be shown in profile, arms and legs must bend, the body must credibly support or be supported by more static objects. The active involvement of the human figure with its surroundings presents new conceptual perplexities of size, distance and perspective generally. Whether to draw only what he sees, or to include also what he knows to be there though hidden—the fourth leg of a table, for example—becomes a practical dilemma for the child; knowledge may still take precedence over immediate sense data, but at least he has become aware that a problem exists. He is now also concerned to achieve a recognisable likeness in his portraits; and in facial expression he will attempt a more varied repertoire than the simple dichotomy between happy and sad which satisfied him at an earlier stage. Age: 8 plus.

Stage VII : Divergence

The problems of concept and technique which arose at Stage VI are particularly difficult for the child to ignore because he is growing rapidly more self-conscious in all his doings. He is vulnerable now to the influence of conventions in drawing, and may become very dissatisfied with his own work if he is unable to produce the highly representational pictures which adults and other children most readily admire. At this point, some children will give up drawing for pleasure altogether. Those who do go on will tend to resolve the problem in one of three ways:

(a) *Development of technical competence*

The conventional resolution is for the artist to forsake his childish spontaneity in favour of learned and highly conscious technical devices: in particular, perspective drawing and the use of shading to give solidity and depth are deliberately acquired. Artistry, in short, enters a cerebral phase. Mastery of these skills not only allows the child to produce an accurate likeness, but gives him the confidence to experiment outside their limitations and eventually to develop his own mature and adult style upon a secure basis. Some children, however, having acquired a little expertise in short-cut methods of slick representation, remain extremely limited in range and produce endless competent but unexciting drawings of fashion models or racing cars, in which they seem content to invest the whole of their talent.

(b) *Neo-primitivism*

Alternatively, the child may now deliberately extend and exploit the naive primitive approach which younger children use spontaneously. Technical devices are largely ignored, but because the child voluntarily rejects these expedients rather than being unaware of them, his pictures become far more controlled and sophisticated. At the same time, they retain a freshness and a quality of simple candour often missing from the drawings of more technically competent children. The "neo-primitive" artist has a sharp eye for detail, colour and decorative effect, together with an unforced sense of balance. Some of the charming naiveties which characterize the work of younger children may persist, but now with an air of stylistic confidence: eyes too high in the head, arms rather short, and children depicted as minute replicas of adults.

(c) *Retreat into facetiousness*

Faced with their own inability to solve the problem of making their pictures look realistic, other children protect themselves from criticism in advance by drawing only in a facetious manner. Genuine representation is abandoned, and novel but rigid conventions or gimmicks are adopted which are intentionally unrealistic, thus neatly sidestepping the issue: faces may be drawn as masks, or the body may be deliberately distorted to bizarre effect. This defensive pose is seen at its most blatant in the use of jokes and visual puns; the child seeks admiration for cleverness rather than artistry.

(From E. and J. Newson, 1966. Introduction to the British Association Exhibition "The Innocent Eye", now available as an illustrated audiotape from the Medical Recording Service Foundation, Kitts Croft, Writtle, Chelmsford, Essex.)

Even a brief examination of the drawings by normal children included here (pp. 99–101) shows that Nadia did not parallel this development. The drawings of normal 6-year-olds are far more schematic and rigid. None of the pictures show the dexerity and reproductive skill which Nadia displayed. Features such as feathers on birds are achieved by patterns; perspective and foreshortening are virtually absent. Mistakes of reproduction are frequent— such as having arms sticking straight out of the chest, or all the legs of the horse completely visible or both legs of the man shown on one side of the horse, etc.

Again, a point where Nadia differed from the normal child is that she did not use "tokens" for objects. There are many examples of this in the drawings of the average 6-year-olds; the sun, and trees are only two examples. These symbols are representations for objects which in the act of drawing form the "language" for this type of expression. Just as words are once removed from reality, so are the symbols of drawing. For Nadia, no such symbolization of the visual world took place.

Her drawings, on the contrary, were marked by inventiveness and experimentation. The ability to generalize and improve showed an extremely rapid progress (although her earliest drawings were skilled from the outset). The techniques of perspective, foreshortening and the use of space were present from the age of $3\frac{1}{2}$–4 years, although perspective usually only develops in early adolescence. It is, in fact, often absent in the drawings of primitives and is regarded as one of the marks of sophistication of mature drawing. The use of colour, how-ever, which usually dominates infant's drawings after the age of 5 years, was totally absent in Nadia's work.

Nadia used shading and shadow from the age of 6. This usually develops at 10–11 years. Her used of space was not dominated by the paper medium—rather she would draw to the edge of the paper, which then truncated the image. The young child is usually dominated by the limitations of the paper and deforms the image to fit it. This usually persists to quite a late stage—and is still present in adult work where emotional considerations—wholeness and completeness can dominate over form. Nadia appeared to be dominated by form.

The normal infant has considerable problems in representing three-dimensional objects in two-dimensions. He draws a table with four legs joining the top section, for instance. He is dominated not by what he sees but by the need to represent the relationships he knows. Nadia, on the other hand, drew what she saw and was uninhibited by the fact that the back legs of an object join the body at some point.*

---

* Graham *et al.* (1960) showed that the tendency to close open figures and to increase symmetry when copying figures declines with age. A series of figures were prepared, consisting of four simple four-sided asymmetrical shapes and four circles or squares with a $\frac{1}{2}''$ gap. Eight children of average intelligence were asked to copy these shapes, after a 10-second presentation, on to paper of the same size as the presentation figure background. Nadia was also presented with this task—and the results were compared. In all cases the quality of Nadia's copies was better. She showed less tendency to close up the gap in the figures and also less tendency to render her figures

Harris (1963) also includes an extensive review of empirical findings on children's draw-ings. McCarty (1924) found that at age 4, 70% of children used outline principally and somewhat less than 30% used mass (where the child means to portray solidity), although there was a steady change towards the use of mass so that by age 8, 60% of the children used mass. Nadia did not demonstrate a steady change to the use of mass and remained dominated by the use of line.

McCarthy (1924) also evaluated the appearance of proportion, balance and perspective all of which were virtually non-existent in drawings of 4-year-olds. Proportion is achieved first and the effective use of relative size among objects is usually achieved by age 8. This was always a distinctive feature of Nadia's drawings. From the age of 4 years her drawings showed proportion. "Balance and symmetry in the arrangement of forms or objects remains quite foreign to 8-year-olds", says Harris. Although we traditionally think of balance and sym-metry as being consciously strived for with the artist rearranging his model or components of his picture to achieve a pleasing effect, Nadia often achieved balance but fortuitously, because her drawings have a photographic quality.

Leroy (1951) found that the use of perspective appears as early as 4 and is reasonably common by age 8. However, Harris disputes this and says that most studies have shown that attempts at perspective are quite infrequent before the ages 11 or 12. Malrieu (1950) found that perspective appears at about age 10 and Harris, in his own study, found very small but increasing proportions of children use perspective after age 10. In Leroy's study, his children were required to reproduce a drawing of a house, car and a boat—three objects where one might expect early attempts at perspective. The three-quarter turned horses Nadia produced in perspective are surely much more difficult to draw?

Ellsworth (1939) found that when design was analysed in drawings of nursery school children, if design was apparent, it most frequently took the form of a simple figural element placed in rows, columns or concentric circles. Nadia's drawings showed no such decorations and again were notable by the absence of this very common trait in children.

Harris draws four main conclusions from the evidence:

> 1. The earliest scribbles are more than random markings. They are patterned by the mechani-cal arrangement of the hand, wrist and arm as a multiple jointed lever; they are probably modified by the scribblers visual observation and to a very limited degree by relations within the drawing field.

In other words, some intentionality can be found in the earliest scribbles of young children. The remarkable fact about Nadia was that from $3\frac{1}{2}$ to 4 years of age she had mastered manual dexterity and was drawing recognizable objects highly competently. The period of practice and mastery was very short and presumably learning took place at a phenomenal rate. Her parents did not remember her scribbling and believed her to have drawn objects from the moment she put pen to paper. However, it is almost inconceivable that she could have drawn without some practice before mastery of the medium.

Another important aspect of Nadia's drawing ability is a consideration of the manual dexterity needed to produce the drawings.

Connolly and Elliott (1972, 1974) have been investigating the development of hand function as expressed in the grasps used by young children. They have studied the mastery of the prehensile potential of the hand and have plotted the development of a general manual skill underlying various manipulative tasks.

They distinguish between two types of grasp; power grasp and the precision grasp. In Nadia's case we are concerned with the precision grasp (or in Connolly and Elliott's terms "intrinsic" movement). They found that in a sample of nursery children of between 2 years 4 months and 4 years 10 months the incidence of grips which allowed intrinsic movements showed an age related increase and that even at 4 years of age the child is still learning to use his hands.

One only has to ask a child of 4 years to draw a straight line between two dots, or draw a circle to realize how wide is the margin of error and how poor is eye-hand co-ordination. The

---

more symmetrical. In all respects her figures were closer to the originals. It could be deduced from this that she was advanced for her age—since the described tendencies diminish with age. A more parsimonious explanation is that she was less influenced by "Gestalt" considerations and more by the true perceptual form of the object.

very young child characteristically proceeds in jerks or small discrete movements, whereby he allows his pencil to move in the general direction, stops and uses his eyes to check the progress, makes the necessary adjustment and proceeds on again. As the child grows older and with massive practice in the acquisition of handwriting skills feedback from eye to hand becomes continuous (Fitts and Posner 1967). Again, Nadia defies what is known about the normal development of eye-hand co-ordination.

> 2. The majority of young children show a common directionality in drawing simple forms. This directionality in the drawing act is probably influenced by components of motor-development. The way the object drawn is oriented on the page is also predictable for most children, and likewise may be related to motor development.

Harris goes on to give details of research findings and he says young children commonly draw both the square and the diamond using four separate lines, and that children usually have a preferred orientation in drawing profiles; in the majority of cases profiles face left. Rouma observed that young children name their first drawings according to fancied resemblances after completion. Nadia used two movements to draw a diamond, and neither of the other points was true of her.

Rey (1947) affirmed that even older children do not draw solely from a mental picture of their subjects but are influenced by the drawing process itself. After a stroke has been made the child artist sees and uses cues in the changed sketch, and thus is progressively guided in making further strokes. The drawing act is thus governed by factors intrinsic to the process. Nadia, however, redrew her line until she found a satisfactory one and was not influenced by her own drawn lines in the manner suggested. She obviously did not name her drawing at any time but almost invariably appeared to have a definite idea about what she was drawing so there were no wasted lines. Frequently the lines she drew did not resemble any object to the onlooker until she added important detail and the whole became apparent—it could then be seen that few of the lines were redundant and it was evident that she had intended the figure from the outset.

Harris concludes: "Although his motor behaviour may guide a child's execution and interpretation of his drawings, his work after the acquisition of speech primarily reflects comprehension and cognition". Meili Dworetzki (1957) concluded that the pre-school child commonly interprets drawings much as he performs them, that is, the same limitations of idea that appear in drawings appear also in children's discussions of the drawings.

This touches on a central issue in Nadia's drawing ability. For what is true in the majority of cases is not true of Nadia. There are numerous examples in her work of the inclusion of details which were beyond and outside her experience, let alone her language and ability to discuss; bridles, straps and girths on horses; epaulettes, braiding and shoulder bags on the riders, for example:

> 3. Children's drawings represent objects as they perceive them. Even the simplest most primitive drawings are wholes, yet contain discernible parts. With increased age this whole or Gestalt quality of drawings shows a progression; it is more detailed and at the same time more complexly organised.

And, later,

> The Goodenough method of scoring drawings has shown conclusively that the representation of features of the human figure increases with mental growth.

If these statements are to apply universally then Nadia must be a child of exceptional intelligence! Age norms in Goodenough's study show that the appreciation of abstract properties of the human figure such as relative size or proportional and spatial relations between parts develops much more slowly than the awareness of the existence of parts. Children depict parts which have a particular significance for them at the time. Nadia's human figure drawings when she was 4 years of age did show a lack of proportion—enlarged head and elongated necks—but by 6 years of age her sense of proportion was very well developed.

Geck (1947) emphasized the importance of kinesthetic experience to visual and auditory impressions as improving the quality of drawings. Geck had students explore manually a human head before sketching it and practical manuals for the training of artists have long stressed this point. Nadia rarely saw and practically never touched the subjects she drew except for human beings.

Barnhart (1942) examined the manner in which space was depicted by children of different ages. At first there is no apparent concept of graphic portrayal of space; objects are scattered at random over the paper. This is followed by a linear form of representation in which objects are arranged in a row usually upon a ground line. Next comes a period of ranked space in which there are two or more rows. The ground lines in the background are either straight or curved to indicate relative distance. This technique shows only a rudimentary idea of perspective. A transitional period follows leading to the final idea of "true space", with recognition of such factors as perspective, partial concealment of objects in the background by those in the foreground, foreshortening and the like. Lowenfeld (1957) also ascribed to these stages of development.

Nadia did not show this normal development pattern and from the age of $3\frac{1}{2}$–4 drew according to the description above of true space; perspective was present in her earliest pictures together with partial concealment, foreshortening and diminution of size with distance.

Several studies where children have been required to draw a model or copy geometric designs have revealed limitations according to age.

Townsend (1951) correlated copying ability with measures of form perception, motor skill and IQ and he concluded that copying ability of children may be much more correlated with form perception than with motor skill.

It is interesting to note that Townsend's findings help to explain Nadia's ability (i.e. that form perception is an essential component of drawing ability) and it is also interesting to note that IQ was found to be less important. Although it would seem that motor ability (manual dexterity) and representation of form are too highly integrated to be separated.

It has been found that when a time interval occurs between viewing a model and making the drawing, systematic rather than aimless modifications take place. Gibson (1950) thought that conceptual materials, in the absence of visual models influence the reproduction of visually perceived forms, and this process follows systematic lines of occurrence. Certainly systematic changes did exist in Nadia's drawings but it is doubtful whether these were of a conceptual nature as understood by Gibson because she had no language and there are other indications of impoverished conceptual development.

The research findings have also shown a tendency to complete figures or reduce ambiguities when copying from memory; as discussed previously, Nadia would complete a headless figure of a horse traced from one of her own drawings but she would also draw human figures without heads.

4. Central or cognitive factors appear to be crucial in determining developmental features of the reorganization of mental life and the dominance of conceptual knowledge over concrete drawing performance.

In a study by Mott in 1945 he was able to show that children's drawings of a man improved after practice at reciting parts of the human body. Similarly, Stotijn Egge (1952) showed in her study of mentally retarded children's drawings that none of her non-performing children (those who could only scribble and not produce a recognizable figure) had language. Golomb (1973) demonstrated that the presentation of verbal instructions enhanced drawing ability in children. She read to children the body parts in order. As early as 1930, Karl Buhler emphasized the verbal rather than the visual representation of reality in a theory which predates Luria by 20 years:

By the time the child can draw more than a scribble, by age 3 or 4 years, an already well-formed body of conceptual knowledge formulated in language dominates his memory and controls his graphic work. The highly schematic drawings of childhood result from this fact. Drawings are graphic accounts of essentially verbal processes. As an essentially verbal education gains control, the child abandons his graphic efforts and relies almost entirely on words. Language has first spoilt drawing and then swallowed it up completely.

Buhler summarized his views, which again are reminiscent of Luria's words:

It is, in the main, language which is responsible for the formation of concepts and therefore for the reorganisation of mental life and the dominance of conceptual knowledge over concrete images.

Despite frequent allusions to the importance of language to the development of conceptual processes and in particular to the supposed parallel development of drawing ability, very little evidence was offered at the time of the study. I therefore decided to test the theory with normal children.

Twelve 4-year-olds, six girls and six boys were selected, all considered to have average IQs by their teacher's rating. The Goodenough and Harris "Draw-a-Man" test was administered to each individually. This was followed by a test in which the children were required to label parts of the human body. The Stanford Binet picture of a little boy was used and I had a prepared list of parts of the human body as follows:

Head	Mouth	Elbow
Ears	Cheeks	Hands
Hair	Chin	Fingers
Eyes	Neck	Thumb
Eye-lash	Shoulders	Legs
Eyebrow	Chest	Knees
Forehead	Tummy	Ankles
Nose	Arms	Feet

This list was concealed from the child.

Each Subject was instructed by the words "We are going to play a game. I would like to see how many parts of this little boy's body you can name. I will point to a part and you can tell me what we call it." The part was then clearly pointed out and each time the naming was prefaced by the question "And what do we call this part?". I found that the children frequently muddled up their labels knowing the word but applying it incorrectly—arm for hand and ankle for elbow. However, the criterion adopted was correct labelling of parts. The total number of the parts of the body correctly named was then correlated with the score obtained on the Goodenough test and a Pearsons Product Moment correlation of 0·9 resulted. The total for naming parts gives both a very crude test of language development—the acquisition of noun substantives, and possibly the degree of differentiation and consequent complexity of concepts which the child has.

From this simple pilot experiment it does appear that drawing ability and linguistic development are highly correlated although of course no causal relationship can be inferred and indeed a higher order factor such as intelligence or conceptual development may be involved.

How did Nadia relate to this whole area of drawing ability and conceptual and linguistic development? Harris states that drawing parallels and reveals conceptual/cognitive development which will be similarly revealed in the language the child uses. As Nadia was mute she certainly did not bear out any direct link between drawing and language.

Buhler's comments are more diffuse and do appear to allow for the possibility of a child such as Nadia, for he suggests that "language swallows up visual perception"; that reality is reorganized upon language development so that the child eventually comes to rely on verbal mediations even for motor and perceptual processes. Nadia may be a rare example of a child undominated by language who found a pure visual and perceptual means of communication or representation.

One of the major assumptions in the foregoing debate from Buhler's work is that language is a prerequisite for conceptual development. This is a debatable argument. Furth (1974) for example, strongly argues that conceptual development can be visual and perceptual at least to the stage of formal operations. Others have argued that although some conceptualization is possible without language, development of abstract concepts would be retarded and restricted. As far as Nadia's conceptual ability is revealed by her drawings, she has shown that "retardation or restriction" are misplaced descriptions. The question also arises as to whether conceptual development (whether perceptual or linguistic in origin) is a prerequisite for drawing.

A hypothesis emerges that in the normal child, drawing ability parallels cognitive and conceptual ability because language predominates as the means for organizing experience. Drawing in the normal child is accomplished by predominately conceptual rather than perceptual means. Goodenough reports, for instance, the well-known fact that the child will not look at a model when asked to draw a man. But verbal labelling as a conceptual process appears to improve drawing ability.

In Nadia's case and in the absence of language development, she drew what she saw untrammelled by conceptual reorganization or verbal mediation. Perhaps this is why she studied and looked so intently at her model.

Comparison with the Drawing Ability of Deaf Children

Harris (1963) provides information on groups who might be thought to parallel Nadia's case. Firstly, Nadia showed many of the characteristics of a profoundly deaf child. How does the deaf child's drawing ability compare with the normal child's? One may expect some compensations on the perceptual side as a result of linguistic impairment and, as with Nadia, drawing ability to be more highly developed than normal. This is a fondly based but false hope. Thiel (1927), on the basis of an examination of nearly 2,000 drawings made by children in schools for the deaf, came to the conclusion that the development of drawing among the deaf parallels that found for the hearing but that progress is slower. Working with a number of tests including the Goodenough "Draw-a-Man" test, Myklebust and Brutton (1953), found a distinct conceptual inferiority for deaf children. And using the McAdory Art Appreciation Test, Pintner (1941) discovered that deaf subjects between the ages of 11 and 21 years performed as well but no better than hearing subjects of corresponding age. Although the deaf girls did slightly better than the boys, they showed no superiority over hearing subjects.

Comparison with the Drawing Ability of Mentally Retarded Children

Nadia showed many of the characteristics of mental retardation. In a comprehensive study of mentally retarded children up to age 14 years in the Netherlands, Stotijn Egge (1952) found the same drawing sequence observed in normal children, in mentally retarded children. However, drawing proceeded to develop at a much slower pace in the retarded children and development was several years behind their chronological age in all cases. She identified a group of non-performing children; those who made no drawings at all. None of these children possessed words. "Scribblers" in every case had a few words, and nearly half of them had speech. All children who achieved recognizable drawings of objects had more or less acquired language. Lobsien (1905) compared the drawings of "imbeciles" with those of normal children and found that age for age the sense of proportion displayed by mentally retarded subjects is decidedly inferior.

Harris says that the drawings of subnormal children tend to be far more primitive than those made by normal children and show many immaturities. Harris continues by saying that this difference has been noticed by many other writers—for example, Cyril Burt (1921) believed that it was possible in most instances to differentiate between the drawings of normal and backward children, by the lack of coherence in subnormal children's drawings.

Rouma (1913) also stated that the drawings of subnormal children resemble those of younger normal children, but he noticed the following special differences.

1. There is a marked tendency to automatism.
2. There is a slowness in the evolution from stage to stage.
3. There is a frequent regression to an inferior stage of the development of drawing.
4. There is a lack of coherence of ideas—for example, the drawings often covered a sheet of paper and were not finished and they had to do with a number of very disparate subjects.
5. Some subnormal children can sometimes draw one or two subjects surprisingly well but when this is investigated it is usually found that the child has confined himself to these one or two subjects which have in fact evolved very slowly.
6. Subnormal children prefer those drawings in which the same movement frequently occurs. And,
7. They usually do very meticulous work.

I approached the Midlands Society for the Mentally Handicapped who hold regular exhibitions of the art work of ESN/SSN children and adults. They kindly allowed me a free hand to examine and photograph any of the pictures in their possession. I examined hundreds of such paintings and drawings. None of the pictures examined showed as high a representational quality as that exhibited by Nadia. Very few were as good as the drawings of normal children of the same age.

Comparison with the Drawing Ability of Autistic Children

I could find no studies about the drawing ability of autistic children *per se*, although Rutter (1970) has shown that they often have a wider spread of abilities and deficits on standard IQ tests than do other subnormal or normal children. Special abilities or "islets of intelligence" are a hallmark of autistic children, although the development of these special abilities rarely proceeds above what is average for ordinary children.

Comparison with Normal Children of Exceptional Ability

Even in normal children an artistic talent or representational ability beyond their years is extremely rare (hence the use and construction of the Goodenough scales). Harris comments that Goodenough was led to an intensive search for talented child artists. She discovered that while child musicians are not at all uncommon, the child artist is indeed a "rara avis". Goodenough's statement is:

> In spite of careful research the writer has been unable to locate a single child under the age of 12 years whose drawings appeared to possess artistic merit of a degree at all comparable to the musical genius occasionally shown by children of this age. Examination of drawings which make unusually high scores on the test leads to the opinion that keen powers of analytical observation, coupled with a good memory for details are more potent factors in producing high scores.

(It should be pointed out that while the "Draw-a-Man" test is used widely as a test of intelligence its correlations with other IQ tests such as WISC; 0·4, Stanford–Binet; 0·7, are only modest whilst test–retest reliability is found to be high.)

From the evidence presented in the foregoing sections it is evident that Nadia was atypical in all four cases; deaf, subnormal, autistic and normal, and this highlights the exceptional nature of the case.

Comparison of Mentally Retarded Children with Special Talents

The terms "idiot savant" or "talented aments" are out of date, often inappropriate, and cover such a wide range of both mental defect and special skill as to be of so wide a generality as to be useless. However, the term "idiot savant" is still employed by Psychological Abstracts and provided the means for a search for similar cases to Nadia.

In many of the cases of "idiot savant" IQs of 60–70 are reported and, in one case, as high as 81. (Wechsler or Stanford Binet scores are invariably given.) Often the cases reported are of adults and only rarely is the child younger than 10 years. Scheerer *et al.* (1945) point out that the diagnosis of subnormality was far less informed in the past than it is today. The so-called "cretin imbecile" painter Gottfried Mind, described by Tregold, died in 1814 when neither endocrinology nor clinical psychology had developed.

Some cases of "talented imbeciles" which were reported were found to be cases of adults who had suffered brain injury and subsequently manifested special ability. Goddard (1916) reported two cases of outstanding drawing ability, but the subjects were later diagnosed as psychotic rather than retarded.

In some cases the reported talent is solely in relation to the subjects' general performance, where the ability comes into relief simply because it exceeds their general mental level but without reaching normal functioning. In other cases the talent is within normal bounds but remarkable for the retarded subject and in some the talent is genuinely exceptional.

I made a thorough search of the literature pertaining to special abilities in subnormal children to find similar cases to Nadia and to try to discover what the incidence of exceptional drawing ability might be. I have already touched upon the fact that Goodenough states that the child artist with outstanding abilities is a rare event, although Rouma suggests that some cases of highly practised drawing of one object can exist in retarded children. It seemed likely that cases of ability as outstanding as that of Nadia would have appeared in the journals although it soon became apparent that idiographic studies of this nature are out of fashion and only a few cases of "idiot savant" have been reported since 1960.

Such cases were far more commonly reported in the 1920s and 1930s; many cases were reported at this time and hence provided comparisons for Nadia. However, not one study was really applicable to her, and as far as I could discover there are no reports of phenomenal drawing ability in a child of Nadia's age.

Tredgold (1937) reports on one most interesting case:

> Occasionally the talent for drawing passes beyond mere picture copying and shows real artistic capacity of no mean order.
>
> The celebrated Gottfried Mind had such a marvellous faculty for drawing pictures of cats that he was known as "The Cats' Raphael". Gottfried Mind was a cretin, deemed to be an imbecile, born at Berne in 1768, where he died at the age of 46 years. At an early age he showed considerable talent for drawing and as it was obvious that he would never be able to earn his living in any ordinary occupation, his father's employer interested himself in providing young Gottfried with some training. He could neither read nor write, he had no idea of the value of money, his hands were remarkable for their large size and toughness and his general appearance was so obviously indicative of mental defect that his walks through the city were usually to the accompaniment of a crowd of jeering children. In spite of all this his drawings and water colour sketches not only of cats, but of deer, rabbits, bears and groups of children, were so marvellously lifelike and skilfully executed that he acquired a European fame. One of his pictures, of a cat and kittens, was purchased by George IV.

Apart from this case, only two other cases* of phenomenal drawing ability were available. These occurred in a long review and detailed study of one "idiot savant" with remarkable ability in numerical calculation (Scheerer *et al.* (1945)). This review gave a critical analysis of cases of "idiot savant" reported before 1945 and mentioned two cases of outstanding drawing ability given by Rothstein (1942). He found eight talented subnormals in a population of 4,000 subnormals.

> Subject D.W. C.A.25. M.A.8 draws and paints landscapes almost exclusively. His spontaneous products give the impression of some artistic ability but on the standardised Lewerenz Test in fundamental abilities of visual art he proves to be inferior to the comparable average adult. . . . Subject F.T. C.A.17. M.A.9 has drawing ability in pencil and crayon. On the Lewerenz Test she scores below average.

However, as these people were all adults, their cases do not parallel that of Nadia. The IQ scores of the latter two cases as judged by their Mental Ages are not in the SSN range and it is reasonable to deduce that language was present as the subjects scored at mental age 8–9 years. Even so their drawing ability does not seem to have been exceptional.

I found many cases of exceptional memorizing ability, arithmetical ability, lightning calculators and musical talents. Many of the cases revealed talent and ability in one area developed well beyond the normal, and in a small number the ability was truly phenomenal. Downey (1926) reports the case of a man who could repeat 27 digits after one presentation of them. Tredgold (1937) observes that in a considerable proportion of "idiot savants" the gift is one of memory in one form or another.

---

* A further case of a retarded boy with exceptional artistic talent was reported in 1976 (Morishma and Brown, 1976). The important difference between this case and Nadia is that the boy's talent was first identified when he was in the seventh grade (at least 13 years of age). Morishma and Brown reported that this boy was retarded in most cognitive functions but that visual perception was average as is the case with Nadia. Another interesting parallel is that Morishma and Brown suggest that this boy has possible damage to the left cerebral hemisphere. See Reynell Language Development Scale results (p. 119).

Theories of the "Idiot Savant"

Among the hypotheses advanced in the literature were the following:

1. Jones (1926) introduces what he calls an "atypical focalized habit system". This may consist of persistence in the preferred line of activity, for example deliberate memorization, or of massive compensation for abnormalities by excellence in one area. This was possible in Nadia's case—although persistence and practice was not typical of her.
2. Brill (1949) invokes unconscious memory or inheritance of acquired characteristics. I suspect that scientists generally would find this explanation as unacceptable as the idea of demonic possession!
3. Jaensch (1930) generalizes the findings in one of his cases of a calendar calculator in postulating eidetic imagery and the use of schematic procedure. His subject reported being able to see the whole calendar before his mind's eye—and read off the date as requested. The possibility of eidetic memory in Nadia's case will be discussed later (see pp. 112–113).
4. Morgan (1936) places the blame for "idiot savants" on "injudicious education", i.e. that those who have in their care someone showing a peculiar aptitude in one direction are apt to give special training in that, to the exclusion of other subjects.
5. Both Tredgold (1937) and Morgan (1936) appear to find the development of one specific talent as leading to imbalance and "furthering autistic withdrawal", although it also becomes the means by which the child receives recognition, attention and praise.

Other writers have entertained the interesting and tantalizing hypothesis that one talent assumes not only the hegemony among all other abilities but crushes them almost to the point of extinction. Intellectual deficiencies in such cases then actually spring from "an excessive intellectual quality and achievement in one direction".

If this were the case one might expect the growth of the particular talent to pre-date the retardation or to develop along with signs of retardation. In Nadia's case the language problem was apparent by the age of 2 years and there was no sign of extraordinary perceptual or motor development then. There are also supremely talented normals whose other intellectual functioning is far from impaired, but rather enhanced by a transfer of learning from the area of their special gift.

Scheerer et al. (1945) conclude that the development of a special talent in the retarded individual is probably due to a conditioning process whereby achievement and competence in one area provide a tremendous degree of motivation for persistence at that skill. However, they also say that the retarded individual is unable to achieve abstract conceptual development and claim that in all cases of "talented imbeciles" the talent remains restricted to the abnormally concrete level.

La Fontaine and Benjamin (1971) in the most recent review of the subject, suggest that in the mentally retarded individual, where one cognitive function only remains intact, the range of stimuli responded to is narrowed and leads to a channelling of responses. The response is narrowed but intensified.

Although all these theories are of interest, at best they are only partial explanations and none gives satisfactory insight into Nadia's level of skill. Nadia appears to be a very rare case indeed, but children with other talents, musical and numerical, have always existed. In the rush to establish general laws of behaviour psychologists have recently neglected such cases, but they have much to teach us.

5

A Consideration of Wider Theoretical Issues

Wider Issues

One of the frequently recurring statements in the literature on children's drawing is that "the child draws what he knows not what he sees." Goodenough and Harris share this view, that the child's drawings are largely governed by what he knows. Goodenough believed that an explanation of drawings by children involved hypothesizing the existence of parallel conceptual development. As has been said, "discriminations and generalization furnish the person with concepts and the means to organize and structure sensory experiences." Goodenough believed that human intelligence and individual differences were manifest in the ability to perform such operations and manipulate the resulting concepts and that this is revealed by drawings.

Goodenough, at the start of her book (1926), states that an explanation of children's drawing must go beyond the fields of simple visual imagery and eye–hand co-ordination and take account of cognitive processes. In order to represent objects by means of drawing the child will have had to consciously analyse the object and to have extracted the elements and features which are essential characteristics. He then has to order these elements spatially. The brighter the child the closer is his analysis of a figure and the greater his appreciation and ability to depict the spatial relationship between the elements. Goodenough continues:

> Backward children, on the other hand, are likely to be particularly slow in grasping abstract ideas. They analyse a figure to some extent and by this means are able to set down some of its elements into an organised whole. But this is likely to be defective and in some instances entirely lacking. It is this inability to analyse, to form abstract ideas, to relate facts, that is largely responsible for the bizarre effects so frequently found among the drawings of backward children.

Harris (1963) explains that concepts become more differentiated as the child increases his contacts with objects under different circumstances and as he discriminates more and more aspects of them. With added experience the child's concepts become increasingly abstract. Children's drawings of the human figure likewise include more abstract elements, such as appropriate proportion of limbs, head, trunk; assignment of the figure to a class through the use of clothing or accessories, the depicting of activity and the like. Modifications are towards increasing elaborations of the basic concept and towards the inclusion of more abstract elements.

Harris continues by saying:

> No data have ever appeared to controvert the general import of Goodenough's observations and conclusions. Rather, the increased body of data serves to fill in the process she outlined. Drawings of objects are based on concepts; concepts are based on experience with objects. Experience increases the aspects of objects to be reacted to, understood and incorporated in drawing.

Not only are the number of these aspects increased by experience, but the relationships among them are grasped more completely. Thus with experience, a larger number of concrete aspects are understood and used in drawings.

The problem here is that no adequate definition of "concepts" is given. Be that as it may, however, it has already been shown that Nadia was capable of highly complex drawings of objects on the basis of very little experience of them (the Pelican drawings for instance), and without the slow differentiation of relationships, detail, etc., Goodenough and Harris describe. However Nadia was drawing, she did not follow the pattern and description given here by Goodenough and Harris.

The question arises again as to whether concepts can be derived from a purely visual analysis such as Nadia appeared to use, or whether concepts, language and experience are all necessary.

The questions remain

1. Is any level of drawing or representation possible without conceptualization and symbolization?
2. Does conceptualization and resulting symbolization interfere with the possibility of representing what is really perceived?

Drawings are abstractions from the real world insofar as they are two-dimensional representations of the three-dimensional world and therefore could be regarded as conceptual. Did Nadia show any other evidence of conceptual development, if indeed drawing alone is not to be taken as evidence. I looked for evidence for this and one significant example exists. When Nadia was required to copy a drawing of a duck she drew three pictures—all of birds and one of a cockerel with pelican's wings (No. 51). This suggests that she had categorized a class of objects—birds. One can therefore conclude that Nadia probably had limited conceptual development and this was probably visual in nature, in the form of images or icons.

In fact, some writers such as Arnheim (1954) and the empiricist psychologists in the field of perception have gone so far as to argue: "One sees only what one knows". Their argument is that perception develops with learning.

Arnheim maintains that perception does not start from the observation of particulars but from generalities. He uses the example of triangles. The child first perceives triangularity; the distinction between individual triangles comes later. He claims, therefore, that early artistic representations based on naive observation are concerned with generalities; this is, with simple overall structural features.

Nadia is of the utmost importance to this debate because she was capable of reproducing and therefore registering detail quite beyond her experience and understanding and conceptual development, at least as revealed by language. She could draw a tongue on a cockerel without knowing the noise it makes or without having seen the living bird! This is much more in harmony with the Nativist perception school and suggests that the receptors are pre-tuned for visual information and that, like a camera, from birth humans register the visual field with all its details but without understanding. However, the issue is not this simple; interpretation and reproduction are also involved. Nadia was not only registering stimuli, she was also reproducing it and in so doing she was interpreting, for she omitted some information and concentrated on other areas. Now the Nativist case is not so plausible for one would have to postulate that Nadia also knew instinctively or innately which parts of the visual display to draw, which constituted a whole and which area of detail (the head and eye) were important and which were not.

The only possible reconciliation which could be forged between strict empiricist theory and the facts of Nadia's case would be to suggest that she had a phenomenal ability for perceptual learning. In either case, the study of Nadia has pointed out the inadequacies and flaws in both philosophical positions.

Gombrich in "Art and Illusion" (1960) discusses the old debates on the psychology of perception and the processes involved in drawing. One of his major conclusions is that "Art is born of art—not of nature". What he has to say about painting is equally applicable to drawing. He quotes from Roland Freart, a sixteenth century art teacher:

> Whenever the painter claims that he imitates things as he sees them he is sure to see them wrongly. He will represent them according to his faulty imagination and produce a bad painting. Before he takes up his pencil or brush he must, therefore, adjust his eye to reasoning

according to the principles of art which teach how to see things not only as they are in themselves, but also how they should be represented. For it would often be a grave mistake to paint them exactly as the eye sees them, however much this may look like a paradox.

Gombrich's point is that representations are grounded on systems which the artist learns to use, and these "techniques" are dependent on the traditions of art, not on visual reality. Gombrich quotes Wölfflin, who said "all paintings owe more to other paintings than they owe to direct observation". Gombrich emphasizes the distinction between perception and representation but at the same time the central paradox is that the drawing accounts for the picture seen just as much as the picture seen accounts for the drawing.

Gombrich maintains that without some previous examples from other artists of the portrayal of spatial relationships and the way visual elements interact, the artist could "never stand on the difficult path of adjusting". He continues:

> The achievement of the innocent eye, what modern authorities call stimulus concentration, turned out to be not only psychologically difficult but logically impossible. The stimulus, as we know, is of infinite ambiguity and ambiguity as such cannot be seen—it can only be inferred by trying different readings that fit the same configuration. The artist has learned to probe his perceptions by trying alternative interpretations.

The artist starts from a schema—usually the point his predecessors had reached in the task of representation, and he strives for corrections which approximate ever closer to the real world. Gombrich says:

> You must have a starting point, a standard of comparison, in order to begin that process of making and matching and remaking. The artist cannot start from scratch but he can criticize his forerunners. The evidence of history suggests that all artistic innovation involves the systematic comparison of past achievements and present motifs.

What Gombrich has to say has to be paraphrased here. His book is long and closely argued and he warns the reader against a cursory analysis or quoting parts of the book out of context. However, again, one has to consider the case of Nadia in the light of these statements. Was Nadia informed by the tradition of art, or does she represent a case of an "innocent eye" upon reality? It does seem likely that she learned much from past attempts at two-dimensional representations of the three-dimensional world by her attention to pictures in books. The case would be quite consistent with Gombrich's statements if she were simply copying pictures. However, she also drew from life and this is more difficult to reconcile with Gombrich's view that ways of representing have to be learned, as her apprenticeship was so short. However, Gombrich does make a very important point in his book that knowing and seeing are logically related and cannot, without distortion and ambiguity, be discussed separately.

An interactionist view is probably closest to the truth. Each individual is the unique product of the interaction between the organism and the environment, but, in most cases experiences and capacities are sufficiently similar for generalizations and predictions to be possible. In a case such as Nadia, some of the laws of human behaviour and their attendant theories are not illuminating.

Eidetic Imagery and Drawing Ability

One of the possible explanations for Nadia achieving such a high level of reproduction was that she could be an "eidetiker".

Individuals with eidetic imagery can retain a visual image for varying lengths of time and it was conceivable that Nadia was capable of holding an image, seen in space before her eyes, and of reproducing it on paper by drawing around it—much like the image produced by an eipidiascope.

Eidetic imagery was once thought to be a normal stage of development in all children and therefore to be related to other facts of early cognitive development, such as sensory rather than verbal modes of encoding experience, and concrete rather than abstract modes of thought. However, recently the question has been raised as to whether eideticism is a normal phenomenon with adaptive significance or whether it is essentially maladaptive and a direct manifestation of brain pathology.

In a study of eidetic imagery among the retarded, Siipola and Hayden (1965) reported that eight out of 16 brain-damaged children possessed eidetic imagery, compared with only one out of 18 familial retardates. In a population of 151 normal primary school children Haber and Haber (1964) had found 12 children who were eidetikers. The incidence of eidetic imagery is, therefore, low; an estimated 8% of the normal child population.

Richardson and Cant (1970) suggest that eidetic imagery may be a normal phenomenon in most children which disappears by the time they are 7 or 8 years old, but some children may have difficulty in processing visual information at higher cortical levels due to brain damage, or an optical defect. They may continue to use the eidetic ability as a high-capacity short-term memory system, but it is essentially a compensatory mechanism. However, Richardson and Cant failed to reproduce the earlier findings of Siipola and Hayden and found only one out of 62 brain-injured subjects possessed eidetic imagery and only three out of 61 normal children.

These statements were of considerable interest with regard to Nadia. The conventional methods of testing for eidetic imagery were not possible in Nadia's case, and the possibility of demonstrating eidetic imagery in a mute and unco-operative child seemed insuperable. We did, however, devise a "matching" test—although the results produced were inconclusive.

The test devised was based on black and white line drawings of 12 common objects. For each drawing on the stimulus array there was a pair of cards showing incomplete tracings of the object, such that if the two cards were superimposed the whole object could be seen. The object was not easily recognizable from either of the two cards viewed separately.

Nadia was given the first card of each pair for 10 seconds; this was then removed and the second card was given—and then removed. Despite the difficulties of motivation and communication Nadia demonstrated clearly that she could match the image she had acquired, after seeing the second card, to the corresponding object, correctly and without hesitation—although in the majority of cases she failed to match the cards presented separately. Although this may well indicate that Nadia possessed eidetic imagery, it is not conclusive evidence.

As previously discussed Nadia paid attention to line and shape and may have found enough information from the lines and general shape on the second card to make an accurate match. The question of eidetic imagery remains open. However, there are other, more fundamental difficulties. Even if Nadia was an eidetiker the problem of finding a satisfactory explanation for her extraordinary ability is not answered. The task of drawing is of a much higher order than merely tracing round an image. The problem is not just of imaging but also of reproducing. The question remains—how did Nadia achieve her interpretations of the originals with their attendant modifications and transformations?

In fact, one of the main conclusions of this study is that in Nadia's case the possession of eidetic imagery would not be enough to explain the existence of her remarkable drawing ability. Her drawing showed not only an imaging ability, but she displayed more interpretation. The original image was placed in a new orientation, details were added or omitted and sizes varied. Nadia showed much experimentation, suggesting that a trial process was being attempted to match the line with the vision, a much more complex process than mere tracing.

Eidetikers are not noted for outstanding drawing ability in general and although imaging must be involved in the drawing process the mechanics of getting that image on to paper are far more complex.

6

Physiological Considerations

It has been the aim of this book to present all the facts about Nadia in a purely descriptive way and not to tie them to any one particular theoretical position too closely. A wide variety of theoretical frameworks are employed in psychology. For example, some researchers use a computer analogy for human behaviour; others use a sociological interpretation, and others a Freudian model. These theoretical frameworks need not be mutually exclusive, but it is important to decide which interpretation of the given facts is the most relevant; which adds most to our understanding of the problem or which model provides most clues for further treatment or remediation.

The approach in this study has been eclectic. But the question of which is the most relevant explanation for Nadia's condition must be considered. Perhaps the model that holds the most attractions as an explanation of the observed facts is the physiological one. It would seem very likely that her unique skill and profound deficits had an organic origin and that she had received some damage to her brain. The treatment of the subject, however, has to be schematic for two reasons: there is very little evidence in this case and no real hard facts and secondly, the physiological literature is very extensive. For the purposes of this book only the most basic and relevant physiological considerations will be discussed.

What are the facts relevant to a physiological explanation?

1. The observed behavioural characteristics and notably her lack of language.
2. There was no evidence of birth trauma.
3. Electroencephlograph Report (10.1.73). Extracts read as follows:

   In addition to muscle action potential, at times some rather irregular activity at 6/8 c/s of about 50 microvolts is seen in both hemispheres mixed with irregular slower and faster components. When she becomes upset there is a slight increase in intermediate slower activity but this subsides quite quickly. The intermediate slow activity is slightly more obvious over the right than over the left Sylvian region and a few sharp elements appear in this area. Responses to photic stimulation are fairly regular and symmetrical, but at rates of about 18 flashes per second a burst of large irregular slow waves mixed with sharp waves occurs generalized. This is repeatable . . . Passive eye closure (accomplished with difficulty) produces some slight increase in arhythmic 11/13 c/s activity at the occiput which diminishes on eye opening. No other short duration spikes were seen.

4. Nadia was lefthanded. She also had one lefthanded sibling. Her other sibling and her parents were all righthanded.
5. Her head shape was brachycephalic. This is unusual in the normal population but frequently found in brain damaged and mentally retarded children. A flattened occiput is often found to be related to language deficits. As a baby Nadia sat up and walked within normal limits and it is therefore unlikely that the flattening of the back of her skull was caused by a prolonged period lying flat.
6. There was some evidence of abnormal substances excreted in Nadia's urine; their

presence might have indicated a metabolic or endocrine disorder. These disorders are not unusual in mentally retarded children. They either have a genetic basis or they can be caused by damage to those areas in the brain which control enzyme and hormone systems.

7. Skeletal and bone age were outside normal limits.

These facts could be regarded as "soft" evidence by neurologists insofar as all of the factors could result from damage to the brain but are not conclusive proof of such damage in themselves. All could occur in a perfectly normal child—for example, 15% of the general population have an abnormal EEG. However, taken together they do present a persuasive picture of brain damage.

It has been shown that brain damage can be caused in a variety of ways. The most vulnerable time for the brain is obviously during birth where compression, differential pressures, oxygen starvation and the tearing of tissue by distortion of the skull can all take their toll. However, the brain continues to be vulnerable throughout life, and in Nadia's case it is also possible that the damage could have been sustained after birth through poisoning by toxic metabolites or by any number of the diseases to which the brain is suspect. If brain damage did occur, and this appears very likely, it is interesting then to speculate which area was affected.

Nadia's most striking deficit was her lack of language. Broca (1865) noted that aphasia (the inability to speak) resulted from a left hemisphere lesion. The Sylvian fissure and its borders are believed to contain the major speech areas and lesions have been located in them in the most long lasting and severe aphasias. It would therefore be reasonable to conjecture that in Nadia the area of most profound damage was in the region of these language centres and adjacent to the Sylvian fissure. This hypothesis is supported by the fact that the EEG Report specifically mentioned an abnormal discharge at the Sylvian region, although the right hemisphere was implicated more than the left.

The abnormal EEG response to fast-rate photic stimulation adds further weight to the brain damage hypothesis and also suggests the possibility of an epileptogenic focus.

The Sylvian fissure is related to the temporal lobe and damage to the language areas would almost certainly involve related structures in this area. A statistically significant number of children with temporal lobe epilepsy, for example, also have speech disorders (Ounsted et al., 1966). Theories of brain damage and resulting language deficits have been thoroughly reviewed elsewhere. One such theory was proposed by Penfield as early as 1954. He was investigating the causes of temporal lobe epilepsy and drew attention to the fact that this whole area appears especially vulnerable to lesions. He and his colleagues suggested that moulding of the head during birth may lead to damage as the temporal lobe is vulnerable to the movement of the plates of the skull. He further suggested that the damage thus caused may be covert. That is to say, that children show no evidence at birth of having received such damage. Penfield claimed to have found evidence of incisural sclerosis in the temporal lobe in his patients and in some who never had "grand mal" epileptic attacks. Creak (1963) has reported that a significant number of autistic children develop temporal lobe epilepsy in their teens. (Temporal lobe epilepsy is significant here only as an indication of damage in this area.)

It seems likely then, that in Nadia's case, on the basis of her EEG report and the shape of her skull, that damage occurred to the temporal lobe area and specifically to the language areas located there.

From the research on language deficiencies the picture is not as simple as presented in the foregoing, because language function is not necessarily tied to the one hemisphere or one location. Perhaps the central problem is that the whole integrated function of the brain produces language or motor skill, for example, and a search for any one area for the location of a function is necessarily doomed to failure. Many other areas of the brain have been implicated in language deficits. Brown and Jaffe (1975) presented evidence which indicated that damage to either hemisphere within the first year of life delays language development. In fact either hemisphere can assume the language function if damage occurs sufficiently early. They support the hypothesis that cerebral dominance (the lateralization of one particular function in one of the hemispheres) is a process that continues to develop throughout life.

Buffery (1972) has claimed that the capacity of the human brain for reorganizing its function after damage is likely to be influenced by the individual's sex. If the right hemisphere is required to subserve linguistic skill following early damage to the left hemisphere, Buffery's theory predicts a slower compensatory development in girls than in boys because of the greater predisposition to left cerebral dominance of language function in the female brain. All this evidence suggests that both hemispheres would have been damaged and such damage is likely to have been diffuse rather than localized in order for no language to have developed at all.

Functions such as language, perceptual skill, etc., are believed to be lateralized in the brain to varying degrees—exactly how this comes about is not known and the main evidence for this arises largely from observations of the loss of functions in people who are known to have received damage to certain areas in the brain. Whether the same applies to a child who never develops these functions in the first place is open to question.

For any proper physiological study of Nadia it would have been necessary to establish the location and extent of the development of these basic functions in her brain. It would have been impossible to get her to co-operate in the standard psychological techniques to determine "brainedness". Another method for determining "brainedness" is the Wada technique of intracarotid injection of sodium amytal (Wada and Rasmussen, 1960). The sodium amytal effectively paralyses one cerebral hemisphere—although again behavioural measures are required to verify which functions are disrupted. To attempt this was well beyond my scope, although the problems of obtaining Nadia's co-operation in normal conditions let alone under clinical conditions, made the problems of an indepth physiological investigation insurmountable.

The remainder of this chapter is concerned with a brief review of the physiological evidence for the location of behavioural functions in the brain and especially those which relate to Nadia.

The physiological view on cerebral dominance has been picturesquely summarized by Levy (1974), and can be paraphrased here. The two cerebral hemispheres are assumed to compliment one another in the integrated functioning of the brain. Each side of the brain is able to perform certain functions which the other side is not equipped to do. The right hemisphere is assumed to "synthesize over space", while the left hemisphere "analyses over time". He goes on to say "The right hemisphere notes visual similarities to the exclusion of conceptual similarities. The left hemisphere does the opposite. The right hemisphere perceives form, the left hemisphere detail. The right hemisphere codes sensory input in terms of images; the left hemisphere in terms of linguistic descriptions. The right hemisphere lacks a phonological analyser; the left hemisphere lacks a Gestalt synthesiser." The right side of the brain while optimally designed for its work, is extremely poorly organized for temporal analysis, abstract conceptualization, detailed feature detection, linguistic coding and phonological analysis. On the other hand, the left hemisphere appears to be very poorly organized for spatial co-ordination. Visual images are fragmented into components and only a small fraction of the information contained in a visual stimulus is extracted.

The description which Levy gives is expounded after a wide examination of a mass of sometimes contradictory experimental evidence. However, the model of a left hemisphere dominant for language and a right hemisphere dominant for perceptual processes is generally accepted. Another important aspect of this is that a strong, though imperfect, correlation exists between cerebral dominance and handedness (Zangwill 1960). The left hemisphere is dominant in language processes in the majority of people who are righthanded and in a smaller majority of those who are lefthanded. Estimates on the distribution of handedness vary, but the most common figure quoted for lefthandedness is 11% (Zangwill, 1960). Estimates on the lateralization of language and perceptual functions are obviously far more difficult to obtain and vary widely, but in the main, studies show that 60% of lefthanders are also thought to be left-hemisphere dominant for language functions, and 98% of righthanders are left-hemisphere dominant for language too. Only a very small proportion of people, therefore, are thought to have language function lateralized in their right hemisphere. This small group of people (of whom Nadia might have been one) are mirror images of the majority of the population. The lateralization of functions are the same—but reversed. Therefore, the claims made in experimental studies still hold for this group. Where the function is assumed to be lateralized on the left it will be found on the right in this small minority and vice versa. As previously mentioned, even the majority of lefthanders appear to have language localized in the left hemisphere. (Goodglass and Quadfasal, 1954; Roberts

1969.) Statistically, therefore, it would be more reasonable to assume that Nadia, even as a lefthander, had language functions dominant on the left side of the brain.

A further confusion to the proposed model is added by the fact that both right and left-handers show different degrees and kinds of laterality effects (Buffery, in press).

Dimond (1971, 1972) criticizes this traditional concept of dominance. He argues that dominance in preferred motor activity cannot directly imply functional dominance. He emphasizes that the hemispheres are not isolated units, and that the control of a hand is not exclusively from the contralateral hemisphere.

As has been stated, we do not know which of Nadia's hemispheres was language dominant and we have no simple means of discovering this. However, it is more probable that language is lateralized in the left hemisphere and the fact that language is absent here suggest that there has been damage to this hemisphere. Lefthandedness in itself can be taken as an indication of damage to the left hemisphere (Levy, 1974). As the majority of people have language and associated motor skill lateralized on the left side and a statistical proportion of people receive birth injuries to the brain where the other hemisphere has to assume functions it can be seen that a greater proportion of people are lefthanded because of brain damage to the left hemisphere.

The speculation that Nadia's sinistrality was the result of brain damage to the left hemisphere would be strong if all her family had been righthanded, but she had a perfectly normal brother who is also lefthanded so that her handedness could be an inherited characteristic and not one which necessarily related to brain damage. Also her EEG recording showed more disturbances in the right hemisphere.

Many studies have linked drawing ability, as a visuo spatial ability, with right-hemisphere function in the majority of people. Although Buffery (1974, 1976) and Kimura (1974) show that the differentiation of the right and left hemispheres with respect to visuospatial ability may be greater for males than for females and the degree of lateralization in individuals varies considerably. It is unlikely that all the components of drawing are lateralized in one hemisphere and McVie and Zangwill (1960) report that left-lesioned patients manifest defects in right–left orientation, sorting objects according to conceptual categories; this also applies to drawing. The drawing defect they note, however, consisted of an over simplification and lack of detail. If normal children draw symbols or concepts and use verbal labels to help them achieve this then these results would not harm the supposition that other components of drawing skill are lateralized in the right hemisphere.

Bogen (1969) presented a summary of disorders following right hemisphere lesions. He quotes the work of Warrington *et al.* (1966) who found disabilities in drawing marked by lack of appropriate form relationships and over-attention to detail. They also noted asymmetries in drawings and a tendency to build up drawings from parts. They further noted particular difficulty in perspective drawing and defects in closure tests.

Kimura (1974) has undertaken an extensive study of the right hemisphere. She states that the right hemisphere is of primary importance for complex visuospatial functions, but also for more fundamental perceptual processes. Functions which are basic to visual perception, such as perception of line orientation, depth perception, rapid scanning of a number of stimuli and visual point location. She concludes that the fundamental processes which she found to be carried out in the brain are the basis for the more complex visuospatial functions attributed to the right hemisphere. She says that though we do not pretend to understand the details, one can readily see, for example, that the accurate appreciation of line slant would be a pre-requisite for drawing a picture.

However, in the same series of experiments Kimura could find no clear lateralization for the identification of a shape and again it would seem unreasonable to expect such a complex process as drawing ability to be lateralized entirely on the right side.

In this chapter some physiological studies which appear to have the greatest significance and relevance to an understanding of Nadia have been considered. Notably, evidence of the lateralization of certain cognitive functions; the effect of brain damage to one of the hemispheres; the relationship between handedness and cerebral dominance and finally some clues as to the aetiology of brain damage and resulting severe retardation.

This survey has by no means been exhaustive and any conclusions with regard to Nadia are extremely tentative, especially in view of the more general reservations expressed in the opening remarks of the chapter.

Certainly an explanation for Nadia's extraordinary drawing ability in terms of brain damage and the compensatory development of the intact areas of her brain remains one of the most attractive hypotheses. But it is one which presents almost insurmountable problems to further investigation.

7

Cognitive Examination of Nadia

As Nadia was mute and many of her social responses were autistic, many of the cognitive tests had to be tried several times before she would co-operate. She would occasionally be very co-operative and at such times she was also far more verbal and used echolalia. On other occasions she was excessively withdrawn. She avoided eye contact and would sit immobile apparently taking no notice of her surroundings.

Non-verbal standardized tests were used but the results have to be treated with caution because firstly she often failed to understand what was required although, had communication been possible, she might have been able to do the tests. Secondly, motivation was variable and there was no means of impressing on her the need for speed. The instruction "Do it as quickly as you can" was superfluous. Also, much of the testing had to be improvised and departed from standard instructions.

The results, therefore, indicated a basal performance of tasks she was capable of performing. However, we had no real indication of ceilings—nor could we conclude specifically that she could not do certain tasks.

Nadia had such a peculiar pattern of abilities, with gross deficiency on the linguistic side and well developed perceptual skill, that any composite result or summation of test items was simply misleading and valueless. There were areas where Nadia scored o (all items requiring a verbal response), and items where she scored at, and above, her age norm. The individual test item, however, had some value in an evaluative capacity and also towards the development of a remediation programme. A thorough use of these tests highlighted areas of deficiency, but more important, areas of competence too. I will therefore give results of individual items in detail, and make little comment on the composite test result.

Reynell Developmental Language Scale (Verbal Comprehension Scale B)

Selective Responses to Word or Phrase

Nadia showed some understanding of simple commands—"Fetch the cup". "Open the door".

Adaptive Response to Familiar Word or Phrase

Again she would respond to simple requests—"Go and sit down". "Stop that".

Looks at One Familiar Object or Person in Response to Naming

Nadia could do this although her lack of co-operation made an overt test difficult. However, in the play situation she would look at her shoe when the word was said.

Test Items

Where is the ball, brick, brush, cup, doll, car, sock etc.? (The subject is required to indicate the appropriate items from a display.) Nadia was unable to indicate recognition of any of these items. However, she did, on other occasions, show that she understood the word "cup". She did not understand the phrase "Where is . . . ?".

    Nadia failed all items in the following sections (3 and 4) and testing was abandoned. The Reynell test was repeated in Nadia's home, her mother conducting the test in Ukrainian, but she showed no more understanding of Ukrainian than of English. Her performance was equivalent to the age level of 6 months.

Pre-requisites of Language Development

Rutter (1972) has outlined a possible test of the pre-requisites of language development. Nadia was tested for these, but as no standardized procedures are available testing was *ad hoc*.

Imitation

Nadia could imitate quite complicated body gestures, such as clapping, tapping her head, crossing legs and tapping alternate feet. These gestures were directed towards herself. However, when gestures were directed at someone else she could, or would not, imitate. She would imitate monosyllabic sounds; te, te; la, la, but would not imitate words of two syllables. She treated the repetition of monosyllables as an enjoyable game but immediately stopped when words of two syllables were introduced. She did not engage in imitative or imaginative games. She used pointing if she needed an object and would lead people by the hand. She could remember where an object had been placed, even if the location was new.

Inner Language

The main evidence that she did have an organized and consistent symbolic system was from her drawings. If she organized her inner world it was evident that little was done through language.

Comprehension of Language and Language Production

The exact extent of Nadia's language was acertained by means of a questionnaire given to both parents and her teacher.

Questionnaire on Nadia

Language (Expressive)

Question	Answer	Details
Can Nadia name or label any items in her environment?	Yes	Few single words: teapot
Using single words?	Yes	spoon
Using two words	Yes	kettle
		horse
		shoe, good
		Nadia, Tania
		(More English than Ukrainian)
More than two words?	No	

Does Nadia have any two-word utterances	Yes	What is it? Shut door; Get up; Naughty Tania; Bed time; good girl
Does she have any appropriate gestures to make herself understood?	Yes	Points to object; points for object without knowing it is there; pulls you for something, e.g. if she wants to go for a walk; gets ready for a walk and points the way she wants to go
Does she ever sing, babble or "la" to herself	Yes	Babbles; sings in rhythm; "talks" to herself without meaning but with rhythm, and intonation—father says she does not concentrate when she does this

Language (Comprehension)

Question	Answer	Details (Complete list)
Does Nadia understand simple commands?	Yes	Put your coat on. Dress yourself. Shoes on. Pick it up. Don't do it. Get out. Go to bed. Go to the toilet. It's bed-time. Daddy's coming. Sit down. Come here. Fetch the teapot.
Does Nadia understand the names of simple objects?	Yes	Fetch the spoon. Eat this. Bring the sugar.
Does Nadia understand simple questions?	Yes	Where is the car?

Motor Development

Question	Answer
Gross:	
Can N Run a few steps?	Yes
,, Jump from one leg to another?	Tries—but rather heavy.
,, Jump with both feet leaving the ground?	Yes
,, Skip?	No
,, Skip with a rope?	No
,, Hop on a preferred leg?	Yes
,, Hop on the other leg?	No
,, Climb up stairs one foot for one step?	No
,, Climb up stairs one step following the other?	Yes
,, Stand up from sitting position on the floor without help?	Yes
Fine:	
Can N Feed herself?	Yes
,, Hold a spoon correctly?	Yes
,, Hold a knife and fork correctly?	Yes—but prefers a spoon.
,, Pick up small items from the floor?	Yes
,, Do up buttons?	Yes
,, Do up buckles?	No
,, Tie shoe laces?	No

Special Language Impairment

We considered the possibility that Nadia was aphasic rather than retarded. Again, no standard testing procedure exists but, if auditory language, reception or expression, or both were impaired Nadia could still have learned through a visual means. I gave her four pictures and four printed word labels selected for being different in outline and length:

duck;   orange juice;   egg;   spoon

I asked Nadia to match the words with the pictures. I demonstrated this to her repeatedly and offered her chocolate for a reward, but she showed little interest. After many trials, conducted over several weeks she showed no learning. A simple receptive or expressive aphasia therefore seemed unlikely and retardation along with motivational and emotional disturbances were again highlighted.

The Columbia Mental Maturity Scale

This test consists of a series of pictures, one of which is different from the rest. It is devised to show the level of conceptual thought of the child through the ability to categorize. The child indicates, by pointing, which item is different from the others. The most successful means of indicating to a non-verbal child what the test requires, is to point to each item saying Yes! Yes! to those which are members of the set and No! to the odd one out. Severely retarded and non-verbal children can manage the test in this manner. Nadia, however, although co-operative on the occasions this was tried, showed no understanding of what was required and her total score was 0.

Merrill–Palmer Mental Measurement of Preschool Children

This proved to be one of the most successful tests with Nadia, due to its many non-verbal items. She failed all the verbal items on the Merrill–Palmer at the first age range 18 months–23 months; she could not obey commands, repeat single words or word groups. However, many of the non-verbal items which needed verbal instructions could be communicated by gestures and Nadia was able to understand what was required. Thus she was able to throw a ball, cross her feet, walk a block along the table and stand on one foot; all problems at the first age range.

She was able to do the Peg Board tasks but did it slowly and deliberately, so failing at 30 months and above. Similarly with the 16 cubes placed in a box task, Nadia arranged each cube with the same coloured face uppermost taking 3 minutes to complete the task and failed to pass beyond 30 months.

With the Decroly matching game, Nadia matched all the items correctly but took a long time over this task—3 minutes, so although she failed at the 60 months criterion on the time limit, she passed on accuracy. She showed her characteristic clumsiness, slowness but persistence, in the button task and started to fail at 42 months criterion.

In perceptual tasks such as the puzzles, she performed best. She passed the Manikin test, Seguin form board, Little Pink Tower and picture puzzles, as well as Mare and Foal at 54 months.

At 60 months, she was able to pass two items out of the seven, these being copying a star and the Mare and Foal Puzzle which she had completed in 47 seconds (the criterion time at this age is 86 seconds or less).

Nadia's copying ability was exceptionally good, as might be expected. She achieved a Raw Score of 47, a mental age of 3 years 3 months.

Other Tests of Mental Maturity

Nadia was largely unco-operative and showed below average performance on all subtests, including those with a perceptual motor bias such as Mazes, Object Assembly and Block Design on the Wechsler Intelligence Scale for Children.*

Frostig Developmental Test of Visual Perception

Nadia proved to be unscorable on this test, although she copied my demonstration. In general, however, her hand–eye co-ordination scores were average.

General Tests

I gave Nadia a wide range of form boards and puzzle toys. She could do complex form boards with ease and showed great persistence. She could also do a form board without having seen the original picture; she used cues of shape and the lines on the piece joining the rest of the form board rather than using cues from the whole picture.

A number of picture-matching games were devised to discover which properties of objects Nadia used when matching. She was very skilled at matching pictures of identical objects. When presented with 12 pictures of the following objects:

table;   chair;   ring;   gun;   walrus;   bucket;   train;   car;   cat;   seal

and 12 cards showing silhouettes of the same objects, Nadia was able to match them without difficulty.

She was then presented with another nine pictures of objects plus 12 miniature objects (taken from the Reynell test) as follows:

table;   chair;   cot;   doll;   ball;   cup;   spoon;   train;   car.

After slight hesitation Nadia was able to match these. She later failed to match 12 object cards to a set of cards showing coloured pictures of the objects but in different sizes or orientations. Normal children had no problems with this test but Nadia could only match three—the table, cat and train. This test was presented to her regularly, but with no success. It seemed, therefore, that Nadia could match on the basis of shape or form—probably using basic perceptual cues: the look of the object rather than what it did or its verbal label. She could also match a concrete three-dimensional object to its picture after some hesitation showing that she could use cues other than basic perceptual ones. She recognized three-dimensional objects from their two-dimensional representation (thus demonstrating that she had some understanding of the reality of the objects she drew).

---

* Luszki (1966) reported on a case of a mentally retarded man who scored very poorly on all the WAIS subtests except for the Block Design, where he excelled. Luszki concluded that of all the regular subtests of the WAIS/WISC only Block Design does not have some specific language characteristic.

> Among other functions, language involves conceptualisation on a semantic basis.

He continues

> semantic conceptualisation is not needed when performing the Block Design subtest. On the Object Assembly subtest for example, each piece of each item is part of a whole configuration which has a definite name and meaning. The person must infer the concept "man", "horse", etc., from the various specific parts and then organize the parts into the figure representing the concept.

This sounds plausible. However, Nadia was nonverbal and she showed no aptitude for Block Design.

She appeared to fail to understand the relationship between pictures of the same class of object. For example, in the final test, two pictures of a chair were presented; one an armchair and the other a wooden kitchen chair. She did not match them. This suggested that her ability to relate objects—to generalize and to form categories—was extremely limited. This conceptual ability is of course a pre-requisite of language. Without recognizing that objects can be classified; that armchairs, deck chairs, kitchen chairs can be subsumed under one label "chair", language development cannot proceed. One can conclude that Nadia experienced increasing problems with matching objects when the possibility of perceptual matching was diminished and abstract, conceptual matching was increased.

8

Conclusions

In psychology, experiments may be devised to establish and elucidate general laws of human behaviour such as the laws of learning. In order to derive a general law, a number of subjects are tested so that an average performance can be obtained and the law so derived can be generalized as widely as possible. This is the nomothetic approach.

On the other hand, it may be that intensive rather than extensive information is required. In clinical studies for example, the more specific the parameters the more precise will be the diagnosis and the treatment. The emphasis is on the individual case and on its uniqueness. This is the idiographic approach.

There is no inherent opposition between group centred and individual centred research although the latter has become unfashionable. Both approaches are necessary although their aims are different. One is directed towards finding general lawful relationships and the other towards describing individual variance. However Chassan (1960) says that while the former has enjoyed favour with experimental psychologists one is unlikely to make important advances in experimental investigation of processes if one ignores individual variance.

An important disadvantage of group studies is that a mean obtained from a group of people may in fact distort and obscure the true state of affairs. Within-subject variance is reduced to zero and so much information is lost. The study of unique and abnormal cases can help to redress the situation. This can establish the generality of the findings and also the tolerance within which the laws apply. Occasionally the unique case can have a more profound effect and calls into question the whole theory if that theory has definitely excluded the possibility of such a case existing.

There are more specific methodological advantages of single case studies. In the first place, with single case studies the specific parameters and accompanying background to the study have been delineated and so many of the usual variables are controlled. Much more can be known about one person than can be known about a group. Also the single case study allows for a longitudinal approach and a careful follow-up over a long period of time is easier. With just one case, the investigator can achieve a much fuller investigation of all the variables in the case and, as he can gather information over a long period, his hypotheses can remain flexible. He can continually review and re-evaluate his subject.

The experimental study undertaken with a group of people and devised to determine a general law allows for the testing of one hypothesis only which is decided prior to the investigation and necessarily limits it from the outset.

Occasionally a case is so unique that only a single case study is possible and Nadia is such a case. The rarity of the case makes it all the more important that an investigation be undertaken. Gregory's study of a man whose sight was restored is another example (1963).

I was extremely lucky to have had the opportunity to study Nadia not just because she was so rare and her ability unique but because she has been important in my personal professional development. I was forced to use an idiographic approach and discovered many of its virtues and I had to take a new look at many of the concepts used by psychologists. I had to apply concepts which I had taken for granted to a real human being. I found great difficulty in defining such concepts as perception, conception, memory and mental image to aid my understanding of this child.

Experimental studies in psychology usually define mental processes in operational terms; learning, for example, could be defined as "the increase in the number of times a lever is depressed". These studies, therefore, confine themselves very narrowly and one danger is that they have an internal logic which shields the student from reality. Not only is there the problem that the laboratory situation may be artificial but there is the danger that mental processes come to be viewed in a narrow and peculiar manner.

A single case study provided me with the perfect antidote. There was no chance of losing sight of the applicability of psychological concepts and laboratory derived laws of behaviour, because Nadia, as a real human being, was always before me. In considering how Nadia learned to draw, lever pressing seems remote and irrelevant and operational definitions fall very short of what we really mean by "learning" in a human being. It is useful to have the perspective of a single case study; the real human being, with which to measure the achievements of experimental psychology.

In this study Nadia was observed in both the home and at school over a period of five months. The policy adopted was to observe the subject's behaviour noting down all the details and then to test hypotheses as they occurred in the process of observing and in reading about theories of children's drawing. The observations were conceived as facts to be defined as exactly as possible and then to be compared and contrasted with theories which already existed.

At the end of the five-month period of observation a considerable amount of information had been collected, and much of this is presented in this book. However, the problem has not been one of data collection but, as with any problem of science, of determining which facts are likely to be important in the investigation. Another psychologist, with his own specialism, or a physiologist or even a sociologist, may object that some essential information has been omitted and a good deal of redundant information included. This is both a fault and a virtue of a "natural history approach". If research is tied too rigidly to one specific theory then one's mind is closed to a consideration of other facts which could lead to another interpretation which might be equally valid and perhaps more relevant. I hope that there will be enough information to allow other psychologists to develop their own theories about this exceptional child.

The important question in this study, put simply, has been to try to determine what is involved in drawing. The following basic plan was suggested as the three pre-requisites for accomplishing a recognizable drawing of an object.

1. Perception; the registration of visual information.
2. Conceptualization; in the form of mental imagery.
3. Symbolization and the external representation of this mental image as a drawing. This would involve eye–hand co-ordination.

Very little has been said about the first process and the question of the relative importance of these three processes and how they interact has not been raised at all. As a result of the predilections of previous writers in the field I have spent most time in discussing some of the issues raised in a consideration of the process of conceptualization.

Nadia lacked the usual means for conceptualizing the external world; language is thought to be the main means of achieving this. Luria (1959) has suggested that words act as tools with which we reorganize and restructure reality. "As a race of people share the same language, they share the same reality." Buhler (1930) has maintained that the acquisition of language exercises a tyranny on the mind. Nadia did not restructure her world through the acquisition of language and yet she was able to show us a level of visual conceptualization through her drawing which, I suspect, would surprise Buhler and Luria!

It is ironic that many artists have claimed that one of the ultimate aims of art is to draw an object as it is perceived, uncontaminated by language or intellect. This brings us back to Gombrich's considerations that children draw what they know not what they see. Nadia, with her extreme impoverishment on both the language and intellectual side drew what she perceived. Like the camera, she recorded a footballer with a massive foot because this was extended towards the viewer—no allowance (and reduction) was made for what she *knew* about the size of the human foot in relation to the human body. This adjustment is automatic in the normally conforming and structured mind.

It is possible to attempt an answer to the questions posed in the earlier chapters on theoretical considerations.

    1. Is any level of drawing or representation possible without conceptualization or symbolization?

Nadia showed us that it is possible to draw without conceptualization, when conceptualization is narrowly conceived as being solely linguistic in nature. However, conceptualization can also be in terms of perceptual and spatial images and Nadia showed us that psychologists such as Luria have underestimated the importance and richness of perceptual and spatial conceptualization. More consideration should be given to the role of perceptual thought, as Furth has stressed.

    2. Does conceptualization and resulting symbolization interfere with the possibility of representing what is really perceived?

It does seem plausible that language becomes a "short-hand for reality" and that with the increasing use of language in the developing child, mental imagery is supplanted and decays through lack of use. This is in accord with the unsubstantiated claim that eidetic imaging is age related.

As language failed to develop with Nadia it is possible that internal visual imagery did not fade but was further developed by her drawing. Conceptualization in the normal child is undoubtedly verbal to a considerable extent. This ability varies between individuals; boys are believed to be better at spatial and perceptual conceptualization than girls, for example. The greater the degree to which the child uses verbal mediation for conceptualizing his world the more likely he will be to use verbally labelled symbols when he draws. It is probable that verbal conceptualization will interfere with the possibility of representing what is really perceived.

Equally important to being able to conceptualize is the ability to get that mental image down on paper. When one considers what is involved in this process it becomes clear that drawing an image which is realistic depends to some extent on the strength with which that mental image is held. If one's own mental image of a horse, for example, is poorly developed; if the image fades or is only seen in the mind's eye fleetingly, it will be difficult to know what to draw, whether the shape is correct and where one has gone wrong. At such times we rely on linguistic labels and draw tokens as a sort of formula to drawing.

For most children the actual process of drawing, of setting down the first line, interferes with the execution of the rest of the drawing. When the first line is put down it becomes the anchor point for the rest of the drawing, all other lines are placed and judged in accordance with it, rather than with the original mental image, if the child held one at all. Nadia drew part of the image over and over again until she was satisfied with the exact position of the line. The ability to retain a good visual image must be part of the answer to explain Nadia's drawing ability. Eidetic imaging was considered earlier but I concluded that this was not the whole explanation. It is possible to comprehend how Nadia could retain a two-dimensional eidetic image of a picture and to represent this on paper. It is much more difficult to understand how she could draw from life and how she could translate a three-dimensional image onto a two-dimensional plane. She mastered all the difficult technical problems of representing depth by perspective. Willats (1977) has examined the development of the ability to use perspective and he has found that the development takes place in discrete stages but that these are related to age. The correct use of convergence to a vanishing point was only mastered by half his subjects between the age of 15–17 years. (Willats uses an analogy between the development of realistic representation by drawing and language acquisition. He quotes Lenneberge who pointed out that the child actively creates and invents language to actualize his concepts. But that language will necessarily be limited by these concepts. This point about language acquisition could equally apply to drawing.)

Nadia's mastery of perceptual relationship is all the more startling and remarkable in the light of Willats comments and findings.

One of the major conclusions of this study is that Nadia's ability, apart from its being so superior to other children, was also essentially different from the drawing of normal children. It is not that she had an accelerated development in this sphere but rather that her development was totally anomalous. Even her earlier drawings showed few of the properties associated with infant drawings. No normal pattern of development was seen; in fact her later drawings did not show a marked progression. Perspective, for instance, was present from the start. From the outset Nadia used a different combination of skills, different cues and responses from the normal child. It would seem logical to suppose that this difference was linked to her deficits in other areas, so that, in Nadia's case, her drawing ability was as much a sign of her abnormality as was her lack of language. One is inclined to think that because Nadia could draw in this remarkable manner that she must have been "intelligent". But her ability was so outside the range of normal activity that comparisons on the basis of such normative and qualitative adjectives are misplaced.

Another tentative hypothesis allied with the foregoing remarks is that Nadia's drawing ability formed some sort of compensation for her lack of language.

The use of the term "compensation" has to be treated with caution. It has occasionally been used to suggest that severely subnormal children are not to be regarded as handicapped or having deficiencies but rather that they are "different". Such a romantic view tries to make an advantage out of deficits. I should like to use the word in a physiological sense. In the flexible and plastic human brain it seems likely that damage or deficit in one area brings about changes in others. If one area is destroyed neuronal connections can be established which can mediate a certain function in another area of the brain. The loss of sight, for example, brings about consequent adaptation in hearing and the loss of a limb causes the other limb to develop muscles to a greater extent than usual.

If Nadia had some form of gross impairment to the acquisition of language it could be that an adaptive response was the development of her perceptual system to a greater degree than normal. The problem here is that one might expect all such children with language impairment to show similar perceptual skills which manifest themselves in drawing ability when clearly they do not. As has been seen from past research, children with language problems do not show an accelerated development of drawing ability. In fact they are usually impaired in this particular respect.

Another area of speculation which has been examined in depth earlier in the book is the likelihood that Nadia was brain damaged and that her peculiar deficits and abilities could be explained physiologically. Although this type of explanation appears attractive the science has not developed to the degree of giving us any great insights into the development of Nadia's drawing ability although physiology can help to throw light on language deficits and related problems.

This study illustrates for me the problems of psychological theory in this area of children's art. As has been demonstrated, some of the most celebrated theories of children's drawing— those of Goodenough, Harris, Arnheim and Gombrich give no great insight as to how Nadia achieved her extraordinary level of skill. The one satisfactory conclusion of this study has been to point out the immense complexity and variety of human behaviour and how far psychology has to progress before an explanation of a child like Nadia can be attempted.

In all respects human behaviour presents the most difficult challenge in the history of science—it is far more complex than the dark side of the moon or the DNA molecule. Nadia remains an enigma.

Postscript by Elizabeth Newson

If, as Lorna Selfe has suggested, Nadia's ability in drawing is inextricably bound up with her failure to formulate concepts verbally, what will be the result of linguistic improvements in such a child?

Nadia entered a school for autistic children at the age of 7 years 7 months, and this postscript is written after $4\frac{1}{2}$ terms' work with her.* She has become more sociable, although her attachments to others, particularly to children, are very obsessional; she appears to gain a great deal of security from the presence of children whom she especially favours, is highly aware of their every action and is distressed by their absence. Her verbal comprehension has improved steadily; she is able to join in certain group games and other activities, and seems to enjoy these. She can obey single-action instructions and a few double-action requests. She has a full understanding of concepts such as big/little, up/down, open/closed.

However, Nadia's expressive language has improved only very slowly. Until recently, she used little speech spontaneously, and this tended to be in the form of single-word utterances, although no longer monosyllabic. Most of her best spontaneous speech has been concerned with children with whom she is obsessed: "Where Martin?" . . . "Give Martin". When distressed she shows considerable delayed echolalia, although this has improved over the last few months. Her teacher reported at age 8 years 10 months that "her awareness of the structure of the school day and its events is greater than her ability to express this verbally, and it is only when there is a change of routine (e.g. a late taxi arrival, or a child absent) that she will spontaneously use speech to note the event".

Within 1:1 teaching sessions, at this age, Nadia's speech was better than elsewhere. She could build up short sentences to describe actions and events, given a visual stimulus. She had successfully acquired use of the pronoun "me", and this had been taught via her self-portrait.

During the term in which she reached her ninth birthday, she was moved into a group of more able and talkative children, and her spontaneous speech has improved. She has begun to ask spontaneously for things she wants, and to use simple sentences, such as "I'd like a plaster, yes, please" when she cut her finger. She has learned to greet people appropriately, rather than echoing "Hello Nadia" when spoken to.

Nadia is coping well with simple number work, and her number concepts 1–10 are well-established. She can manage simple addition and subtraction, and has begun working with money. She is making progress with reading and writing: she can now orally construct simple sentences to describe pictures that she draws, and will then copy-write them, and read them back with understanding.

Sadly, Nadia seldom draws spontaneously now, although from time to time one of her horses appears on a steamed-up window! If asked, however, she will draw: particularly, portraits of the 30 or so adults and children in the school. These portraits may or may not be posed (though she gives little attention to the sitter), and they are recognizable likenesses; in her most productive period, between six and seven, she drew only two portraits from life, and those barely recognizable. In style, Nadia's portraits are much more economical than

---

* I am indebted to Derek Wilson, psychologist at Sutherland House School, for use of his notes on Nadia.

her earlier drawings, with much less detail (see Drawings 108 and 109); often they have a Thurberesque quality. Occasionally, Nadia has produced at home a drawing that shows traces of her original interests (see 107); the one we include here, the most complex she has done since she started school, is no more than a reminder of her earlier horsemen. The fact that Nadia at eight and nine can produce recognizable drawings of the people around her still makes her talent a remarkable one for her age; but one would no longer say that it is *un-believable*.

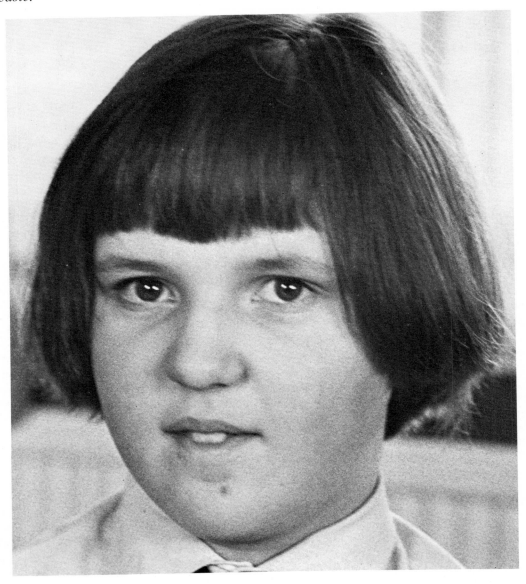

Nadia aged 9½ years. Photograph Sam Grainger.

Is this a tragedy? For us, who love to be astonished, maybe. For Nadia, perhaps it is enough to *have been* a marvellous child. If the partial loss of her gift is the price that must be paid for language—even just enough language to bring her into some kind of community of discourse with her small protected world—we must, I think, be prepared to pay that price on Nadia's behalf.

107

In the original drawing the face of the right-hand figure is coloured in purple, with the features showing through in black. This figure is holding a trumpet with the mouthpiece at his lips. The bell of the trumpet reaches the face of the left-hand figure but the features show through. Note how the middle widens into the bell. The rim of the trumpet is drawn by two concentric circles—i.e. it is a front view compared with side view, no. 27. This drawing is only a reminder of her earlier horsemen.

Here is Derek

Here Derek

This is Miss Stafford

This is Miss Stafford

Two "Thurberesque" drawings of Nadia's classmates.

References

Arnheim, R. (1954). "Art and Visual Perception". University of California Press, Berkeley, California.

Barnhart, E. N. (1942). Developmental stages in compositional construction in children's drawings. *J. Exp. Educ.* **11**, 156–184.

Brill, A. A. (1940). Some peculiar manifestations of memory with special reference to lightning calculators. *J. Nerv. Ment. Dis.* **92**, 709–726

Bogan, J. E. (1969). "The Other Side of the Brain". p. 11. Bulletin of the Los Angeles Neurological Societies, 34, 4, 191–220.

Brown, J. W. and Jaffe, J. (1975). Hypothesis on cerebral dominance. *Neuropsychologia* **13**, 107–110.

Buffery, A. W. H. (1974). Asymmetrical lateralisation of cerebral functions. *In* "Hemisphere Function in the Human Brain". (Dimond, S. and Beaumont, J. Eds.) Elek Science, London.

Buffery, A. W. H. (in press). Sex differences in the neuropsychological development of verbal and spatial skills,

Buffery, A. W. H. and Gray, J. A. (1972). Sex differences in the development of spatial and linguistic skills. *In* "Gender Differences: Their Ontogeny and Significance", (Ounsted, C. and Taylor, D. E. Eds.) Churchill Livingstone, London.

Buhler, K. (1930). "The Mental Development of the Child". Routledge and Kegan Paul Ltd., London.

Burt, C. (1921). "Mental and Scholastic Tests" (3rd Edn). Staples Press, London.

Chassan, J. B. (1960). "Research Design in Clinical Psychology and Psychiatry". Appleton Century Crofts, New York.

Connolly, K. and Elliott, J. (1972). The evolution and ontogeny of hand function. *In* "Ethological Studies of Child Behaviour" (Blurton Jones, N., Ed.) Cambridge University Press, Cambridge, England.

Creak, M. (1963). Schizophrenia in early childhood. *Acta Paedopsychiat.* **30**, 42.

Dimond, S. J. (1971). A reappraisal of the concept of cerebral dominance. *J. Motor Behav.* **3**, 57–62.

Dimond, S. J. (1972). "The Double Brain". Churchill Livingstone, London.

Downey, J. E. A. (1926). A case of special ability with below average intelligence. *J. Appl. Psychol.* **10**, 519–521.

Elliott, J. and Connolly, K. (1974). Hierarchical structure. *In* "The Growth of Competence". (Bruner, J. S. Ed.) Academic Press, London and New York.

Ellsworth, F. (1939). Elements of form in the free paintings of twenty nursery school children. *J. Gen. Psychol.* **20**, 487–501.

Fitts, P. M. and Posner, M. I. (1967). "Human Performance". Brooks/Cole Belmont, California.

Freeman, N. (1976). *J. Ch. Psychol. Psychiat.* (In press.)

Furth, H. G. (1973). "Deafness and Learning. A Psychosocial Approach". Wadsworth Pub. Comp., California.

Geck, F. J. (1947). The effectiveness of adding kinesthetic to visual and auditory perception in the teaching of drawing. *J. Educ. Res.* **41**, 97–100.

Geschwind, N. (1974). The anatomical basis of hemispheric differention. *In* "Hemisphere Function in the Human Brain". (Dimond, S. and Beaumont, J. Eds.) Elek Science, London.

Gibson, J. J. (1950). "The Perception of the Visual World". Allen and Unwin/Houghton Mifflin.

Goddard, H. H. (1916). "Feeblemindedness". Macmillan, New York.

Golomb, C. (1973). Children's representation of the human figure, the effects of models, media and instruction. *Genet. Psychol.* Monograph **87**, 197–251.

Gombrich, E. H. (1960). "Art and Illusion". Pantheon Books, New York.

Goodenough, F. (1926). "Measurement of Intelligence by Drawings". Harcourt, Brace and World, New York.

Goodglass, H. and Quadfasal, F. A. (1954). Language laterality in lefthanded aphasics. *Brain.* **77**, 521–548.

Graham, F. K., Berman, P. W. and Ernhart, C. B. (1960). Development in preschool children of the ability to copy forms. *Child Developm.* **31**, 339–359.

Gregory, R. L. and Wallace, J. G. (1963). Recovery from early blindness—a case study. *Exp. Psychol.* Monograph 2.

Haber, R. N. and Haber, R. B. (1964). Eidetic imagery: I. Frequency. *Percept. Mot. Skills* **19**, 131–138.

Harris, D. B. (1963). "Children's Drawings as Measures of Intellectual Maturity". Harcourt, Brace and World, New York.

Jaensch, E. R. (1930). "Eidetic Imagery". Kegan Paul, London.

Jones, H. (1926). Phenomenal memorising as a special ability. *J. Appl. Psychol.* **10**, 367–377.

Kimura, D. and Durnford, M. (1974). Normal studies on the function of the right hemisphere. *In* "Hemisphere Function in the Human Brain". (Dimond, S. and Beaumont, J. Eds.) Elek Science, London.

LaFontaine, L. and Benjamin, G. (1971). Idiot Savants; Another view. *Mental Retardation* **9**, (6), 41–42.

Leroy, A. (1951). Representation of perspective in the drawings of children. *Enfance* **4**, 286–307.

Levy, J. (1974). Psychobiological implications of bilateral asymmetry. *In* "Hemisphere Function in the Human Brain". (Dimond, S. and Beaumont, J. Eds.) Elek Science, London.

Lobsien, M. (1905). Kinderzeichnung und Kunsthanon, *Z. f. pad. Psychol.* **7**, 393–404.

Lowenfeld, V. (1957). "Creative and Mental Growth". (3rd Ed.). Macmillan, New York.

Luszki, W. A. (1966). An idiot savant on the WAIS. *Psychol. Rep.* **19**, 603–609.

Malrieu, P. (1950). Observations on some free drawings of the child. *J. Psychol. Norm. Path.* **43**, 239–244.

McFie, J. and Zangwill, O. L. (1960). Visual constructive disabilities associated with lesions of the left cerebral hemisphere. *Brain* **83**, 243–260.

McCarthy, S. (1924). "Children's Drawings". Williams Wilkins, Baltimore.

Meili Dworetski, G. (1957). "The Image of Men in the Conception and Representation of Children". Verlag Hans Huber, Bern.

Morgan, J. J. B. (1936). "The Psychology of Abnormal People". Longmans, Green, New York.

Morishima, A. and Brown, L. (1976). An idiot savant case report: A retrospective view. *Mental Retardation* **14**, 46–47.

Mott, Sina M. (1936). The development of concepts: a study of children's drawings. *Child Developm.* **7**, 144–148.

Myklebust, H. P. and Brutton, M. (1953). A study of the visual perception of deaf children. *Acta Oto Largyn. Stockh.*

Ounsted, C., Lindsay, J. and Norman, R. (1966). "Biological Factors in Temporal Lobe Epilepsy". Heinemann, London.

Penfield, W. (1954). Epileptogenic lesions. *In* "Colloque sur les Problemes d'Anatomie Normale et Pathologique Posés par les Descharges Epileptiques". Brussels, Editions Acta. med. Belg., p. 75.

Pintner, R. (1941). Artistic appreciation among deaf children. *Amer. Ann Deaf.* **86**, 218–224.

Rey, A. (1947). The use of drawings as measures of mental development. *Arch Psychol. Genève* **32**, 145–159.

Richardson, A. and Cant, R. (1970). Eidetic imagery and brain damage. *Austral. J. Psychol.* **22**, 47–54.

Roberts, L. (1969). *In* "Handbook of Clinical Neurology". Vol. IV. (Vinken, P. J. and Bruyn, G. W. Eds.) North Holland Publishing Co., Amsterdam.

Rothstein, H. S. (1942). A study of aments with special abilities. Master's thesis. Columbia University.

Rouma, G. (1913). "The Child's Graphic Language". Misch. et Thron, Paris.

Rutter, M. (1966). "Early Childhood Autism". (Wing, J. K. Ed.) Pergamon Press, Oxford.

Rutter, M. (1970). "Infantile Autism". Churchill-Livingstone, London.

Rutter, M. (1972). *In* "Young Children with Delayed Speech". (Rutter, M. and Martin, J. A. M. Eds.) Heinemann, London.

Scheerer, M., Rothmann, E. and Goldstein, K. (1945). A case of "idiot savant". *J. Gen. Psychol.* **66**, 259–300.

Siipola, E. M. and Hayden, S. D. (1965). Exploring eidetic imagery among the retarded. *Percept. Mot. Skills* **21**, 275–286.

Stotijn-Egge, S. (1952). "Investigation of the Drawing Ability of Low Grade Oligophrenics". Luctor et Emergo, Leiden.

Thiel, C. (1927). An investigation of the drawings of deaf and dumb children. *Z. Kinderforsch.* **33**, 138–176.

Tolman, E. C. (1959). Principles of purposive behaviourism. *In* "Psychology, A Study of Science". Vol. 2. (Koch, S. Ed.). McGraw-Hill, New York.

Toulmin, S. (1953). "The Philosophy of Science". Hutchinson. London.

Townsend, E. A. (1951). A Study of copying ability in children. *Genet. Psychol.* Monograph 43, 3–51.

Tregold, A. E. (1937). "A Textbook of Mental Deficiency". Wm. Wood, Baltimore.

Turner, M. (1967). "Psychology and the Philosophy of Science". Appleton Century Crofts, New York.

Wada, J. and Rasmussen, T. (1960). Intra carotid injection of sodium amytal for the lateralization of cerebral speech dominance. *J. Neurosurg.* **17**, 266–282.

Warrington, E. K., James, M. and Kinsbourne, M. (1966). Drawing disability in relation to laterality of cerebral lesion. *Brain* **89**, 53–82.

Willats, J. How children learn to draw realistic pictures. *Quart. J. Exp. Psych.* (In press.)

Wöfflin, H. (1952). "Classic Art". Trans. P. Murray, London.

Zangwill, O. L. (1960). "Cerebral Dominance and its Relation to Psychological Function". Oliver and Boyd, Edinburgh.